NATURAL SCIENCE 1

WELCOME TO CAMBRIDGE NATURAL SCIENCE

Course objectives

- The *Cambridge Natural Science* course has been designed specifically to follow the **LOMCE**. It takes learners on a journey as they discover the wonders of biology, chemistry and physics. Pupils are introduced to topics at a manageable pace, so they can engage with, enjoy and fully assimilate new concepts.
- Pupils learn about and cement their understanding of new concepts through **projects**. In some units, there are projects that run through the unit and pupils review and expand upon the concepts presented. In other units, pupils are presented with different mini-projects to practise and further develop the content at hand.
- Pupils also engage with Natural Science in a **hands-on** way by conducting **experiments**. This practises **critical-thinking skills** and collaborative learning.
- Pupils learn about new concepts through discovery. In *Cambridge Natural Science*, **learner autonomy** is encouraged through the inclusion of interesting facts and thought-provoking questions. Our aim is for pupils to be inspired by the fun and wondrous world of Natural Science.
- **Collaborative learning** is also encouraged through the projects and mini-projects which pupils carry out in pairs, in groups and as a class.
- The course provides pupils with the **linguistic support** that they require to study Natural Science in a second language. The course helps pupils develop their speaking, listening, reading and writing skills. The unit projects and mini-projects give pupils practice of a range of skills and sub-skills.
- Pupils are also given the opportunity to **review the grammar structures** presented in ***Cambridge Life Adventures***. There are links between the two courses that allow pupils to review Science content in English class and grammar structures in Science class.
- *Cambridge Natural Science* is further linked to *Cambridge Life Adventures* in that it provides pupils with practice of the **Cambridge English Qualifications for young learners**. Level 1 provides practice of *Pre-A1 Starters* question types.
- **Mixed-ability assessment** provides teachers with support for pupils of different levels within the same class. It focuses on lower- and higher-order thinking skills, as well as critical thinking.
- *Cambridge Natural Science* has been developed around the key **competences** stipulated in the LOMCE. The course aims to help pupils develop the following key competences: linguistic competence; mathematical competence and basic competences in science and technology; digital competence; learning to learn; social and civic competences; initiative and entrepreneurship; and cultural awareness and expression.

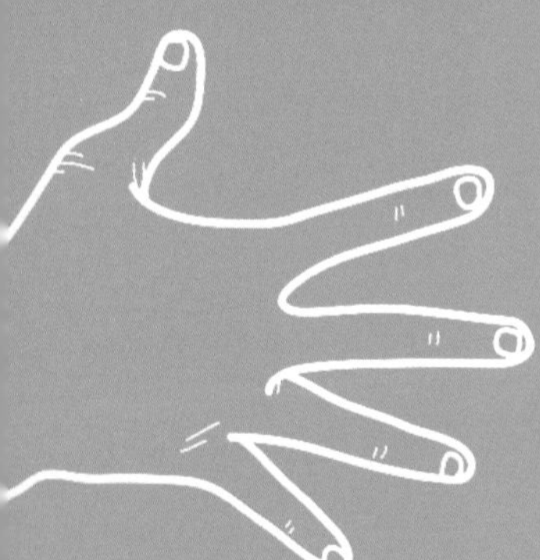

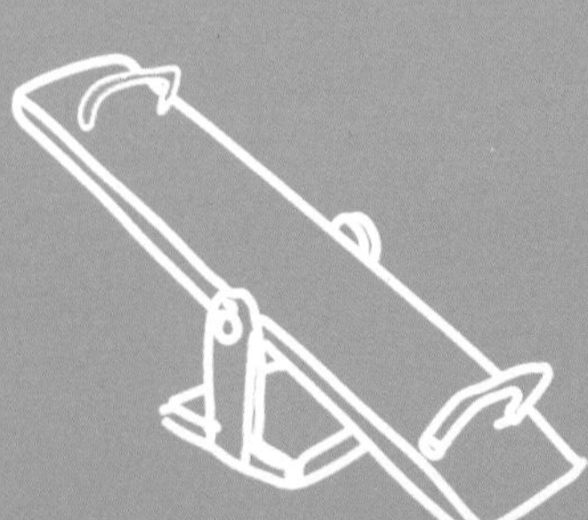

Course components

Pupil's Book: each unit includes a unit project or different mini-projects, experiments, mixed ability assessment and practice of the Cambridge English Qualifications for young learners.

Activity Book: each unit includes activities that consolidate and expand upon the concepts introduced in the Pupil's Book, practice of the Cambridge English Qualifications for young learners and a bilingual glossary.

Class audio: provided through the *Digital Lab*, as well as being available to download online at www.thecambridgeteacher.es.

Teacher's Book: includes useful suggestions for activities at each stage of the lesson, answer keys, audio scripts and track numbers for the audio.

Test Generator: allows teachers to build their own tests for each unit, term and end of year assessment.

Digital Lab: includes an interactive, digital version of the Pupil's Book with a variety of features to help pupils cement their understanding of key concepts:

- flashcards in digital format
- answer keys
- audio with scripts available
- documentary videos for each unit to engage the pupils in a visual way and allow them to see Natural Science in action!

Digital Resource Bank: includes mixed-ability tests, project evaluation grids and curriculum evaluation grids. They are available online at www.thecambridgeteacher.es.

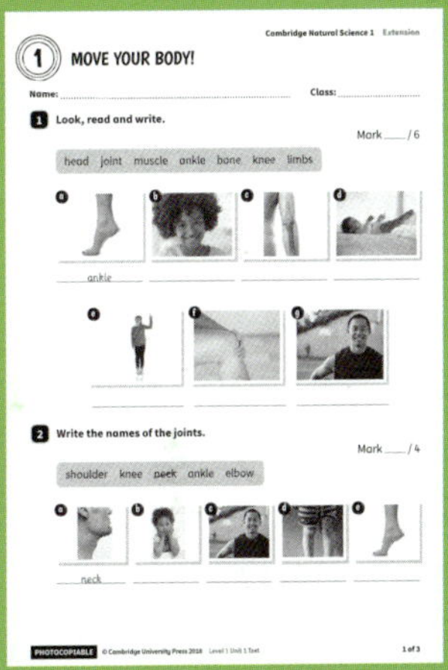

Classroom materials: include posters and a full bank of flashcards to be used across levels. Suggestions for flashcards to use in each unit are provided in the Teacher's Book. The posters consolidate learning by helping pupils engage with Natural Science vocabulary and concepts in the classroom.

MEET OUR SCIENTISTS
PAGES 4–5

Objective:

Pupils will meet the characters that represent each unit of the book. Through them they will become familiar with the main topics and skills that they will study. By discussing the images and text on these pages, they will become curious and engaged with the study of Natural Science. They will see how they too become scientists as they predict and experiment their way through the book and record their journey with their *passport*.

Key vocabulary

animals, family, food, friends, living things, plants, sport, the human body, x-ray

Warm up

Write on the board: animals, friends and family, plants, sport, the human body, in different colours. Ask pupils to give you some examples of each – for the human body, elicit parts of the body. Then say, e.g. *I like animals. What do you like? Tell a partner.*

Main concepts

- Look at the page and ask pupils *What is a scientist?* Elicit that scientists like to discover new things and solve problems by doing experiments. (This is a broad, general description!)

I can think, predict, experiment, observe and conclude. **I am a scientist too**!

Scientific method:

1 Predict
2 Experiment
3 Observe and conclude

Scientist card

Print your finger here when you complete a unit.

Name:

Age:

Welcome Unit	Unit 1	Unit 2	Unit 3	Unit 4	Unit 5	Unit 6

What do you like? Circle.

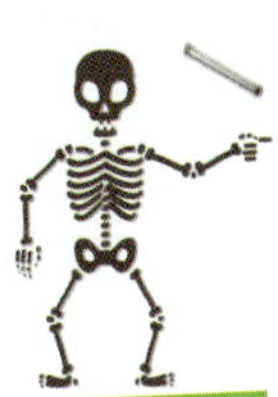

bones and skeletons

plants

healthy food

sport

family

friends

- Point to each character in turn and have pupils point too. Say *What's the name of the character? What does he/she like?* Ask *Which words tell you what he/she likes?*
- Ask pupils to look at the boy with the flower. *What is he doing?* Elicit the process from pupils and highlight the *Scientific method.*
- Ask pupils to circle the topics they like.
- Explain that as they finish a unit, they will put their fingerprint in the passport.

Learn more

- Write on the board, *I'm ____. I like …* Give an example and encourage pupils to write and draw their own sentence and picture in their notebook or on a piece of paper.
- Encourage pupils to practise saying their sentence and to show and tell a classmate.

1

MOVE YOUR BODY!

Learning objectives

By the end of this unit, your pupils will have achieved a greater understanding of the following concepts:

- the three main body sections and the external parts of the human body
- what muscles, bones and joints are
- the five senses and their corresponding organs

Competences

This unit covers the following competences:

- Linguistic competence
- Mathematical competence and basic competences in science and technology
- Digital competence
- Learning to learn
- Cultural awareness and expression

Key vocabulary

Parts of the body: ankle, bone, elbow, hip, joint, knee, muscle, neck, shoulder, wrist

Main body sections: head, limbs (arm, bottom, fingers, foot, leg, toes) torso (tummy)

Parts of the face: cheeks, chin, ears, eyebrows, eyelashes, eyes, mouth, nose, tongue

Five senses: hear, see, smell, taste, touch

Cambridge English Qualifications practice

You will find *Pre-A1 Starters* activity types in the following exercises:

Pupil's Book, Page 79, Activity 2 – Reading and Writing Part 3

Activity Book, Page 4, Activity 6 – Reading and Writing Part 3

Throughout this unit, you will find the following *Pre-A1 Starters* vocabulary:

arm, body, ear, eye, face, foot/feet, hair, hand, head, leg, mouth, nose, person/people, see

Materials needed for *projects:*

- Skeleton worksheet (download from Digital resource bank), split pins
- Mini book worksheet (download from Digital resource bank), photos of pupils' faces

Materials needed for *experiment*:

- Lemon peel, mint leaves, an onion, an orange, liquid soap, vinegar

Materials needed for other activities:

- A selection of fruit

Experiment

The *experiment* provides your pupils with the opportunity to explore their sense of smell by mixing together different items. Pupils will use the scientific methods of prediction, experimentation and conclusion. In addition, they will get creative by mixing different products to create their own potions.

Mindful time

Each unit has a mindful time feature that encourages pupils to relate learning to their feelings and emotions, their relationships with classmates, and their well-being.

In this unit, pupils focus on their breathing and connection to the world around them. An audio track *(track 02)* is available to introduce the breathing activities.

Digital Lab +

- Interactive activities
- Flashcards: parts of the body, parts of the face
- Song: *Body parts*
- Chant: *Five senses*
- Video documentary: *Incredible bodies*

UNIT 1
PAGES 6–7

Objective:

Pupils will talk about parts of the body, the five senses, and identify feelings using a birthday party as a backdrop. They will connect previous knowledge with new concepts.

Key vocabulary

birthday party, body, dance, happy, sad

Warm up

- Ask pupils to think about their last birthday party and tell another pupil: *Where did you celebrate it? Who was at the party? What was your favourite present?*
- Ask pupils to look at the scene and describe what they can see. Encourage them to use the structure *I can see …*

Main concepts

- Ask pupils *What do you think we are going to learn about in this unit? – We are going to learn about the body.*
- Ask individual pupils to read out the questions on the page and elicit answers. Then, ask pupils to read out *Hello! I'm Little Franklin. I'm six today*. Ask them to raise their hands if they are six.
- Ask other questions about the scene: *Who is looking at the presents? – Little Aristotle (is looking at the presents)*. Ask pupils if they would like a piece of the cake and what they think it tastes like.

Little Franklin, Little Curie, Little Darwin and Little Pasteur (are happy).

Little Curie and Little Franklin (are dancing).

Little Linnaeus (is sad).

Mindful time

Ask pupils to pay attention to how they breathe in and out, and how the air travels to their tummies. Ask pupils to sit or stand with a straight back, shoulders down and to breath in through their noses and out through their mouths, deeply, to their tummies, three times. The audio *(track 02)* can be used to help create a feeling of calm.

The audio (track 02) can be used throughout the course to achieve moments of calm, in which pupils focus on their breathing and connect with the world around them.

Learn more

- Sing the song *Body parts* with actions.
- Ask pupils to point to different objects in the scene: *Point to the …* table, lamp, presents, sofa, pizza, balloons, window, cake, rug, etc.

Song
The song focuses on different parts of the body and their movement.

Documentary
The documentary focuses on internal and external parts of the body including bones, muscles and joints. It also covers the five senses.

UNIT 1
PAGE 8

Objective:

Pupils will learn the difference between bones, muscles and joints. They will be able to identify the principal joints in the body.

Key vocabulary

ankle, bones, elbow, hip, joints, knee, muscles, neck, shoulder, wrist

Tip

Play *Simon says* — asking pupils to move different joints. Then, pupils take turns to call.

Warm up

- Do the Mindful time activity.
- Ask pupils *How do you move your body? What's inside your body?*

Main concepts

- Ask pupils to read and say the names of the joints. Then, ask them to point to their own joints and say the names. They can observe the differences between bones, muscles and joints by feeling their own arms or legs. Demonstrate for pupils.
- Read the Fun Fact. Explain as necessary.

Learn more

Pique pupils' curiosity by asking *We know the smallest bone in our body, but which is the biggest? – Femur.*

Bones are hard.

ARE BONES HARD OR SOFT?

Find out

Point to your joints. Practise saying them.

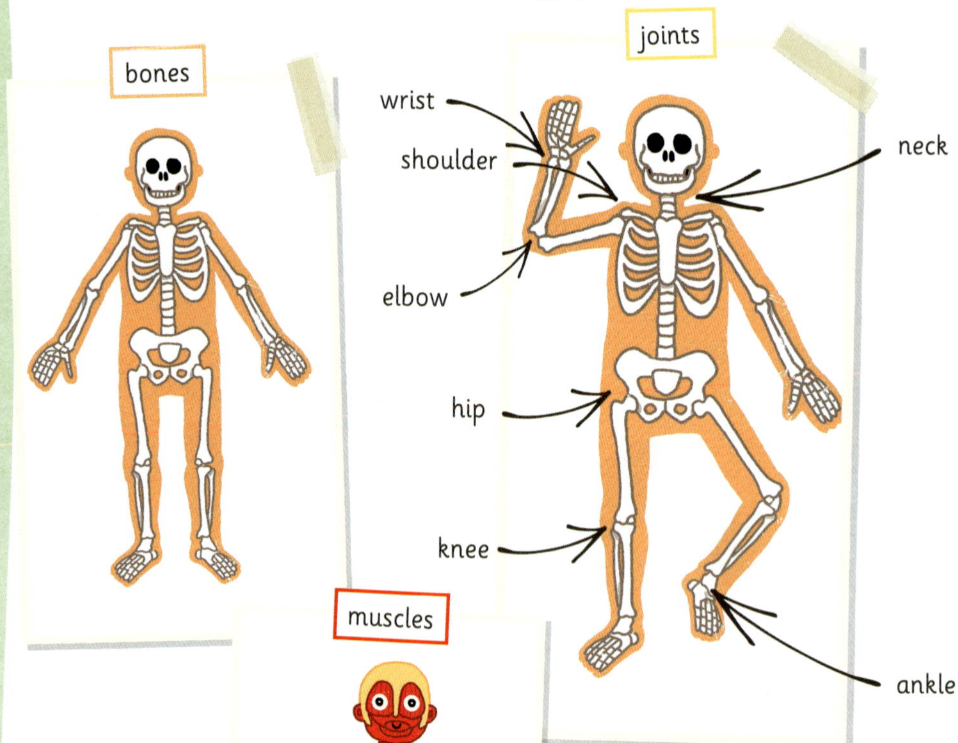

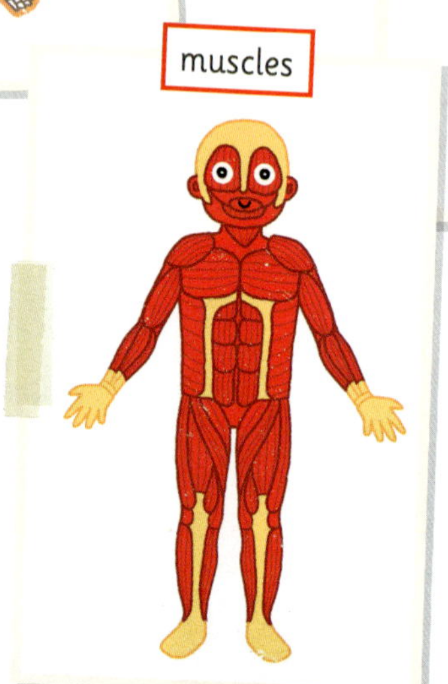

FUN FACT
The smallest bone in the body is in the ear.

8

bones

Mini-project

Try it out

What's in the box?

1 Bones! Build a skeleton. Connect the bones.

2 The skeleton needs joints. Work together.

What have I learnt?

B__________ are hard.

J__________ and m__________ help us move.

My a__________ and my k__________ are joints.

My Dictionary

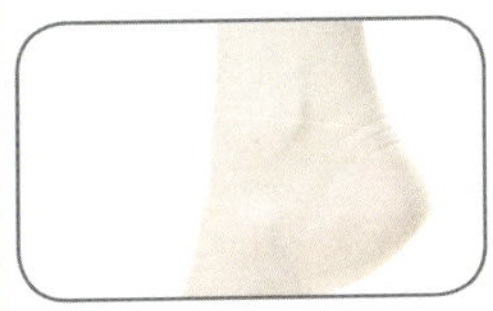

ankle

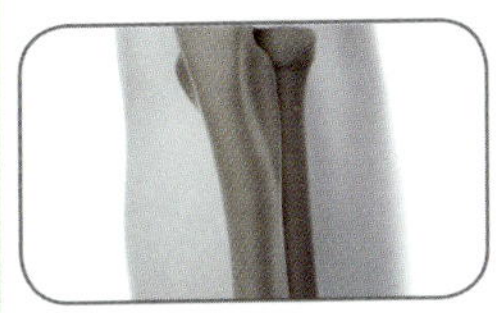

bones

joints

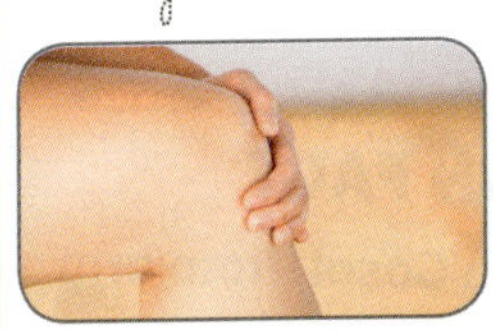

knee

muscles

Bones are hard. Joints and muscles help us move. My ankles and my knees are joints.

UNIT 1
PAGE 9

Objective:

Pupils will understand how bones and joints work together.

Key vocabulary

ankle, bones, joints, knee, muscles

Warm up

Show pupils the box and ask *What's in the box?* Give pupils time to guess and answer, then provide clues, e.g. *They are hard*. Open the box and show pupils what's inside.

Main concepts

- Say *Let's make a skeleton! How can we put it together?* If pupils suggest using glue, glue a pair of arm bones together and show them that they don't move. After taking pupils' suggestions, say *It needs joints.* Show an example.
- Ask pupils to cut out and make their own skeletons using the template.
- Ask pupils *What would happen if we didn't have joints?* Ask pupils to move their bodies without using their joints.

Learn more

- Read *My dictionary* as a class. Ask pupils to find the sticker and trace the words.
- Ask pupils to read and complete the *What have I learnt?* box individually.

UNIT 1
PAGE 10

Objective:

Pupils will identify and locate parts of the body.

Key vocabulary

arm, bottom, fingers, foot, head, leg, limbs, toes, torso, tummy

Warm up

Point to different parts of your body and ask pupils to name any that they know. Then, point to and name all the parts. Pupils copy your actions and repeat the words.

Main concepts

- Ask pupils to read the lesson title and the words for parts of the body. Draw their attention to the different colours for the head, torso and limbs. Ask *What are limbs? – Arms and legs*. Point to the lesson title and ask *Can you answer the question now?*
- Read the Fun Fact. Clarify the meaning of *wide* using gestures and/ or illustrations.

Learn more

- Ask pupils *Can you remember the names of the joints in your leg? – Knee, ankle.*
- Sing the song *Body parts*.

I have got four limbs.

HOW MANY LIMBS HAVE YOU GOT?

Find out

Point to the limbs.

FUN FACT

Pau Gasol, from arm to arm, is wider than he is tall.

10

Mini-project

Try it out

Let's make a Body mini book.

1 Write your name and stick your photo on the cover!

2 Colour your muscles, your bones and your joints. Use a different colour for each.

Fold the page to make your mini book.

MY DICTIONARY

arms

head

legs

limbs

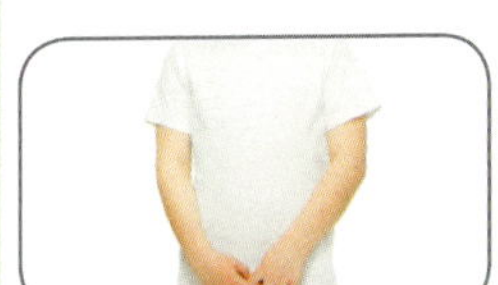

torso

What have I learnt?

My body has got three sections:

a h______________ , t______________

and l______________ .

A______________ and l______________

are limbs.

My body has got three sections: a head, torso and limbs. Arms and legs are limbs.

UNIT 1
PAGE 11

Objective:

Pupils will consolidate their understanding of the differences between bones, joints and muscles. They will recognise the three sections of the body and the limbs.

Key vocabulary

arms, bones, head, joints, legs, limbs, muscles, torso

Warm up

Display pictures of a head, two arms, a torso and two legs. Ask pupils to position them correctly to make a body. Then, they name each part.

Main concepts

- Say *Let's make a Body mini book!*
- Pupils cut out and glue photos of themselves on the cover and write their names. They draw and colour the bones, muscles and joints.
- In pairs, pupils look at each other's mini books and try to remember the names of any bones, muscles or joints.

Learn more

- Read *My dictionary* as a class. Ask pupils to find the sticker and trace the words.
- Ask pupils to read and complete the *What have I learnt?* box individually.

UNIT 1
PAGE 12

Objective:

Pupils will identify parts of the face and head, including the sense organs.

Key vocabulary

cheeks, chin, ears, eyebrows, eyelashes, eyes, mouth, nose, tongue

Warm up

Draw a big circle on the board. Ask individual pupils to come up and draw the parts of the face that they can name in English. Add the names to the picture.

Main concepts

- Read the lesson title as a class and elicit the answer. Ask pupils about eye colour, e.g. *What colour are your friend's eyes?*
- Say words 1–9 and ask pupils to repeat.
- Ask *Which words haven't got a line? – Nose, mouth.* Ask pupils to draw.
- Read the Fun Fact. Explain as necessary.

Learn more

- Ask *Can you remember where the smallest bone is? – The ear.*
- Point out and read together the hidden feature instruction. Pupils find the nose.

No, they aren't.

ARE ALL EYES BLUE?

Find out

Draw the missing lines.

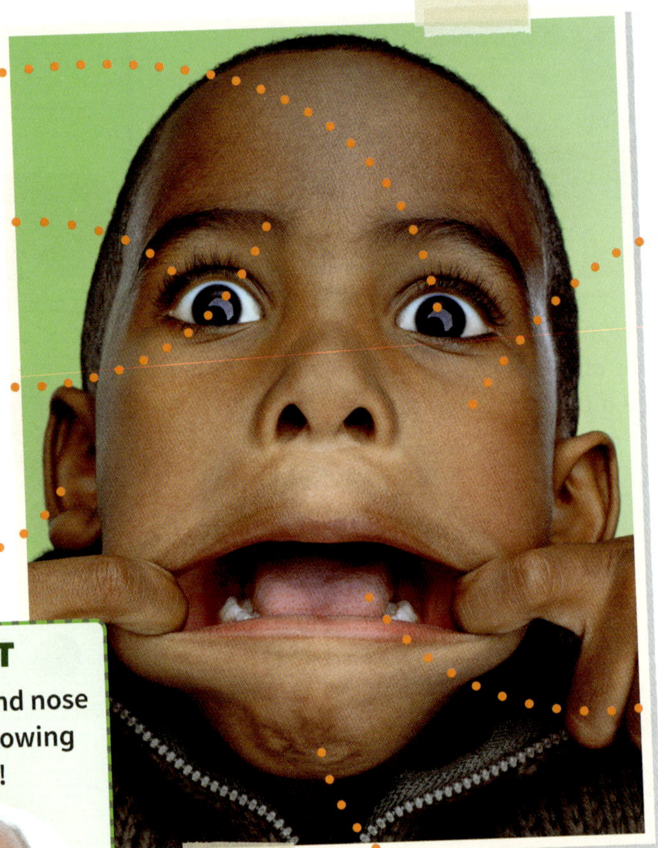

FUN FACT

Your ears and nose continue growing all your life!

Find an animal's nose hidden in the unit!

12

An elephant's trunk, above the Fun Fact on page 14.

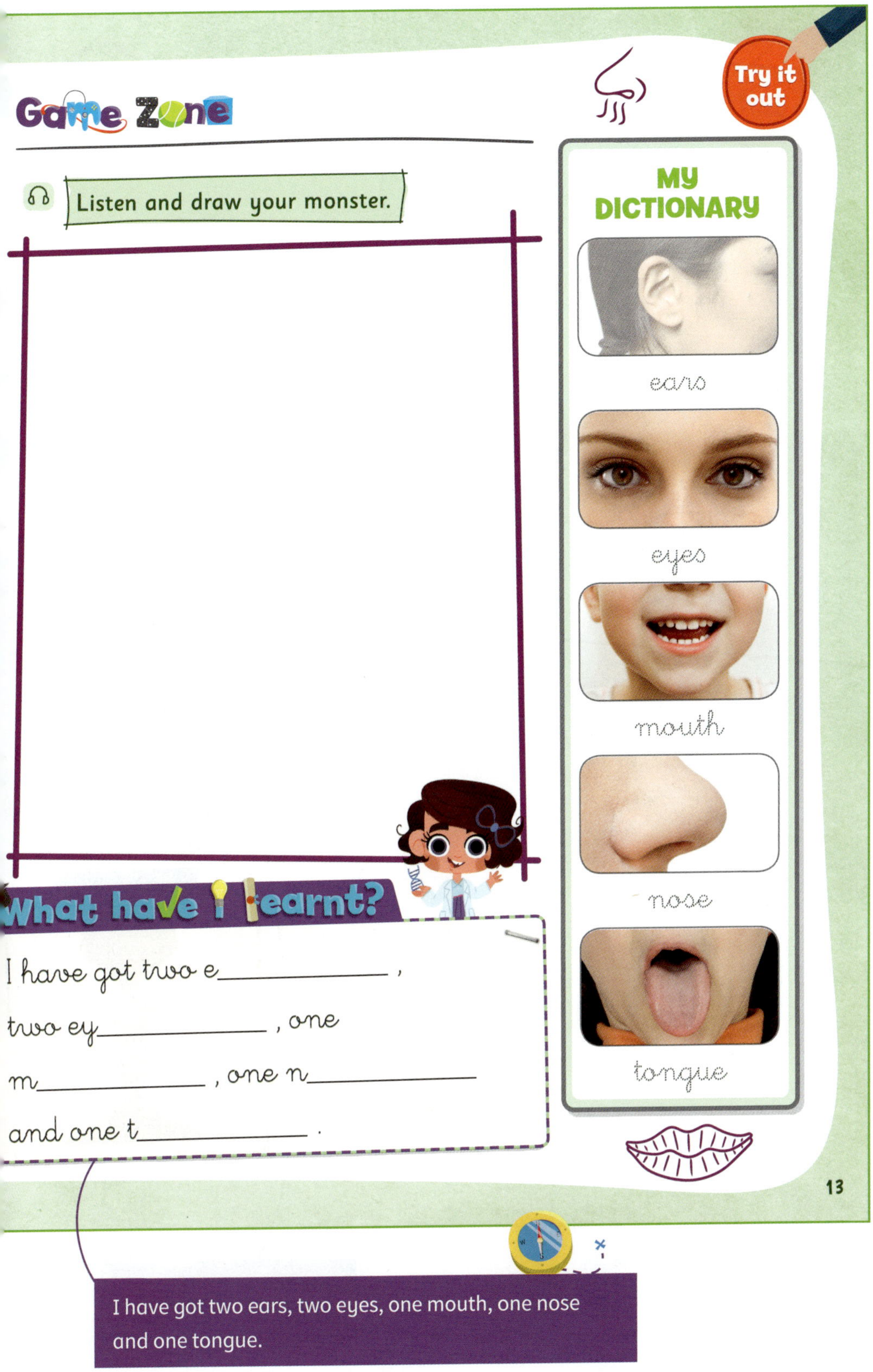
Game Zone

Listen and draw your monster.

Try it out

MY DICTIONARY

ears

eyes

mouth

nose

tongue

What have I learnt?

I have got two e______________ ,
two ey______________ , one
m______________ , one n______________
and one t______________ .

13

I have got two ears, two eyes, one mouth, one nose and one tongue.

UNIT 1
PAGE 13

Objective:

Pupils will listen to and understand a description.

Key vocabulary

ears, eyes, mouth, nose, tongue

Warm up

- Do the Mindful time activity to aid pupils' concentration.
- Play the *What's missing?* game. Draw a face on the board with no eyes. Ask pupils *What's missing?* Repeat with the other sense organs.

Main concepts

- Look at the instructions together and explain that pupils should draw and colour the monster's face according to what they hear. Play the audio twice, pausing as necessary.
- Put pupils in small groups. Give each group a sheet of paper and ask them to draw their own monster. One pupil from each group tells the class about their monster.

Learn more

- Read *My dictionary* as a class. Ask pupils to find the sticker and trace the words.
- Ask pupils to read and complete the *What have I learnt?* box individually.

UNIT 1
PAGE 14

Objective:

Pupils will learn about the five senses.

Key vocabulary

hear, see, smell, taste, touch

Warm up

Play *I spy with my little eye … something big and green/white. – The board.* Invite pupils to continue the game. Then ask *Can you play this game with your eyes closed? – No, we can´t.* Explain that we need our eyes to see.

Main concepts

- Ask pupils to close their eyes. Say *Listen. What can you hear?* Ask *What did you use to listen?*
- Give pupils something to smell. Ask *How does it smell?* Ask *What did you use to smell?*
- Repeat with taste (be aware of allergies) and touch.
- Ask pupils to trace the words. Say the words and have pupils repeat.
- Read the Fun Fact. Accept pupils' answers.

Learn more

Create a Senses corner in the classroom. In a box, place different items to stimulate the senses, e.g. books, rattles, scent, salt, fabrics.

No. You need light to see.

Suggested answers: I can see a glass/cup/two faces.

Experiment

Try it out

Make a potion. Use your senses.

1 Cover your eyes and smell each ingredient.

2 Mix three of the things together. Then, smell the potion.

Conclusion

How does it smell?

UNIT 1
PAGE 15

Objective:

Pupils will carry out an experiment using their sense of smell. They will describe and analyse different smells.

Key vocabulary

lemon, mint leaves, onion, orange, soap, vinegar

Warm up

Show pupils the items they will smell – but they shouldn't smell them. Elicit the item names. Ask whether they think each one will smell good or bad, but don't confirm or deny.

Main concepts

- Go through the first instruction with the class. Ask pupils to work in groups. They close/cover their eyes, in turn, and guess what each item is.
- Ask pupils whether their predictions in the Warm up were correct.
- Go through the second instruction with the class. In their groups, they choose three things to mix together in a potion.
- Ask *How does it smell?* Pupils tick the relevant box.

Learn more

Pupils can repeat the experiment at home using different items and bring their conclusions to school to share with their group.

UNIT 1
PAGE 16

Objective:

Pupils will consolidate their learning through the movement of their bodies and use of the five senses.

Key vocabulary

parts of the body and the five senses

Warm up

Do the Mindful time activity. Repeat as necessary until pupils are calm and focused.

Main concepts

- Do the yoga positions and ask pupils to follow you. Do them slowly, holding each position for several seconds.
- Ask pupils *How are you feeling? Which parts of the body did we move?*
- For Activity 2, ask pupils to cover/close their eyes and give each a piece of fruit. Ask them to feel it, smell it, listen to it and, finally, look at it. Then, they take a bite, chewing slowly before swallowing it. Pupils then talk about the experience of eating this way.

Learn more

Encourage pupils to practise this attentive attitude with other actions such as having a shower or brushing their teeth. They can share their experiences in the next class.

Suggested answer: arms, legs, muscles, joints, etc.

Attitude is everything

1 Do yoga with your teacher. Which body parts are you using?

2 Mindful practice. Eat using your five senses.

16

1 leg	2 finger	3 tummy	4 head
5 arm	6 hand	7 bottom	8 foot

Now I know

Assessment link Go to page 78 for more activities.

1 Listen and number the body parts.

2 Draw a line from the organ to the sense.

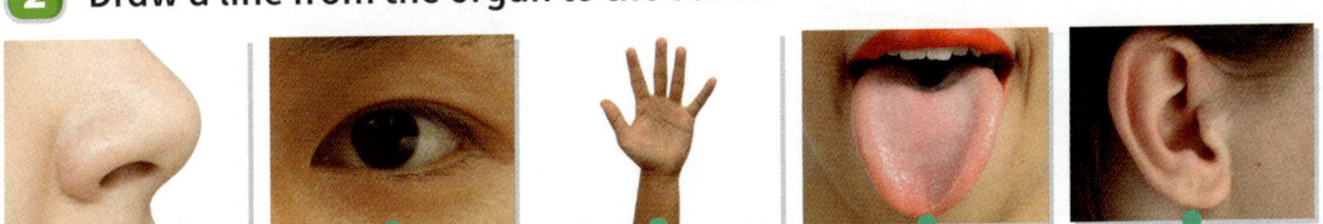

smell | taste | see | hear | touch

Chant Five senses

I am Rosalind Franklin.

I studied the human body.

17

UNIT 1

PAGE 17

Objective:

Pupils will review the content of the unit and read about Rosalind Franklin.

Key vocabulary

parts of the body and the five senses

Warm up

Everyone sings the chant and the song from the unit. Ask pupils to stand up and do the actions together.

Main concepts

- Read the instructions for Activity 1 with pupils. Ask pupils to complete the task. Play the audio twice, pausing as necessary.
- Ask pupils to compare their answers in pairs before checking answers together.
- Read the instructions for Activity 2 with pupils. They complete the task in pairs.
- As a class, look at the photo of Rosalind Franklin and read the information.

Learn more

- Use the internet to look for more information about Rosalind Franklin.
- Go to page 78 for more activities.
- Pupils can now put their fingerprint in the passport on page 5.

UNIT 1 LET'S REVIEW PAGE 78

Find the right words **answers**

1

a This is

b This is

c These are

d These are

2

a What are these? They are eyes.

b What's this? It's a nose.

c What's this? It's a chin.

d What are these? They are ears.

e What are these? They are eyebrows.

Look back **answers**

1

a smell

b taste

c hear

d see

e touch

2

a muscle

b joint

c bones

MEET OUR SCIENTISTS TRACKLIST

Track 01 Page 4, Meet our scientists

UNIT 1 TRACKLIST

Track 02 Page 6, Mindful time
Track 03 Page 7, Song *Body parts*
Track 04 Page 8, *Are your bones hard or soft?*
Track 05 Page 10, *How many limbs have you got?*
Track 06 Page 12, *Are all eyes blue?*
Track 07 Page 13, Listening activity
Track 08 Page 14, *Can you see in the dark?*
Track 09 Page 17, Listening activity
Track 10 Page 17, *I am Rosalind Franklin.* Character
Track 11 Page 17, Chant *Five senses*
Track 54 Page 78, Listening activity

2

STAY STRONG, LIVE LONG!

Learning objectives

By the end of this unit, your pupils will have achieved a greater understanding of the following concepts:

- the different food groups
- the benefits of a healthy diet
- the importance of eating five times a day and choosing healthy snacks
- adopting healthy habits related to physical exercise, rest and personal hygiene

Competences

This unit covers the following competences:

- Linguistic competence
- Mathematical competence and basic competences in science and technology
- Digital competence
- Learning to learn
- Social and civic competences
- Cultural awareness and expression

Key vocabulary

Food groups: carbohydrates, dairy, fats, fruit and vegetables, proteins

Meals and health: breakfast, dinner, healthy, lunch, snack, unhealthy

Healthy habits: heart, keep fit, muscles, sport

Cambridge English Qualifications practice

You will find *Pre-A1 Starters* activity types in the following exercises:

Pupil's Book, Page 29, Activity 3 – Reading and Writing Part 3

Pupil's Book, Page 80, Activity 1 – Reading and Writing Part 2

Pupil's Book, Page 81, Activity 1 – Listening Part 3

Activity Book, Page 10, Activity 5 – Reading and Writing Part 1

Activity Book, Page 11, Activity 7 – Reading and Writing Part 3

Throughout this unit, you will find the following *Pre-A1 Starters* vocabulary:

apple, banana, bread, breakfast, chocolate, dinner, drink, eat, egg, fish, food, fruit, lemon, lunch, pear, pineapple, potato, rice, sausage, sweet(s), tomato, water

Materials needed for *projects*:

- Photos from food magazines/food brochures with different types of food, notebooks
- A soft ball

Materials needed for *experiment*:

- 3 eggs, 3 bowls, water, cola, vinegar

Materials needed for other activities:

- Pictures showing human emotions, a ball of wool, tempera paint

Experiment

The experiment provides your pupils with the opportunity to think about the importance of dental hygiene. Pupils will use the scientific methods of prediction, experimentation and conclusion. They will also learn about process, as they will have to wait for the result.

Mindful time

Each unit has a mindful time feature that encourages pupils to relate learning to their feelings and emotions, their relationships with classmates, and their well-being.

In this unit, pupils learn how contracting and relaxing their body parts can help them feel calm.

Digital Lab +

Interactive activities

Flashcards: food groups, exercise

Song: *I like healthy food!*

Chant: *Be healthy*

Video documentary: *Healthy habits*

UNIT 2
PAGES 18–19

Objective:

The opening spread will allow pupils to learn about different types of food and identify healthy snacks. They will connect previous knowledge with new concepts.

Key vocabulary

carrots, food, fruit, healthy, juice, milk, sandwich, snack, unhealthy

Warm up

Play a short game of *Hangman* using the word *food*. Then, ask pupils to think of all the words they know for food. Write them on the board.

Main concepts

- Ask a pupil to read the title. Then ask pupils to look at the photos. Ask *What do you think we are going to learn in this unit? – We are going to learn about food.*
- Ask the first question to the class *Can you see any food?* Accept answers. Tell pupils to ask each other the second question *What is your favourite snack?* After pupils have responded, give them the opportunity to say their favourite snack out loud to the class. Add anything new to the words on the board.
- Say *Look at the picture. Who is not feeling well? – Little Darwin. What is the matter with him? – He has got a*

I can see apples, bananas, (a bottle of) juice, (a bottle of) milk and sandwiches.

My favourite snack is (pupils' own answers).

Mindful time

This Mindful time activity focuses pupils' attention on their different body parts and the muscles. Pupils should either stand up or lie down (lying down can help to relax pupils and create calm). Show pupils how to contract then relax each of the muscles in the body, starting from head to toe or vice versa. Ask pupils if they feel calmer. They can also integrate their breathing techniques from Unit 1.

stomach ache. Why do you think he has got a stomach ache? Accept all suitable answers.

- Ask pupils to read the speech bubble text. Check comprehension and explain the concept of *healthy*, e.g. *It means that it is good for you*. You can add examples, such as: *Sweets are not good for you. They are unhealthy; Fruit is good for you. It is healthy*. Use gestures if necessary, e.g. thumbs up/down; smiley/sad face.

Learn more

Use the words that you wrote on the board earlier. Ask different pupils to come to the board and circle the healthy food in green and the unhealthy food in red.

Song

The song focuses on eating healthy or unhealthy food and its consequences.

Documentary

The documentary focuses on healthy living, including the different food groups and lifestyle activities.

UNIT 2
PAGE 20

Objective:

Pupils will learn about food groups.

Key vocabulary

carbohydrates, dairy, fats, fruit and vegetables, proteins

Warm up

Books closed. Show pictures of food from the different groups. Check pupils know what they are. Say *Let's classify the food*. In groups, ask pupils to decide which food should be grouped together. When they have finished, elicit the reasons why they chose those groups.

Main concepts

- Pupils open their books and look at the different food groups. Write the names of the food groups on the board and ask pupils to reclassify the pictures from the Warm up. If possible, allow pupils to stick the pictures on the board under the correct group name.
- *Ask Are tomatoes fruit or vegetables?* As pupils give their answers, ask them why they think that.
- Read the Fun Fact.

Learn more

Ask pupils to think about which food group they eat the most of and tell another pupil.

No, they aren't.

They are fruit.

pictures of food

Project Step 1

What's in the box?

1 Food! Classify it into groups.

2 Make a food diary. Draw what you had for breakfast this morning. Which food groups does it belong to?

What have I learnt?

There are five food groups:

1 ______

2 ______

3 ______

4 ______

5 ______

There are five food groups: carbohydrates, dairy, fats, fruit and vegetables, proteins. (in any order)

Try it out

My DICTIONARY

dairy

fats

fruit and vegetables

carbohydrates

proteins

21

UNIT 2
PAGE 21

Objective:

Pupils will reinforce their knowledge of the food groups in Step 1 of the project.

Key vocabulary

dairy, fats, fruit and vegetables, carbohydrates, proteins

Warm up

Show pupils the box and ask *What's in the box?* Give pupils time to guess and answer, then provide clues, e.g. *You can eat it.* Open the box and show pupils what's inside.

Main concepts

- Say *Let's make a poster!* Pupils work in small groups. Give each group a set of pictures and a large piece of coloured card. Ask them to classify the food in the five groups, on each poster.
- Read the instructions for Activity 2 with pupils. To check comprehension, ask a pupil to tell the rest of the class what they must do. Pupils start a food diary in their notebooks.

Learn more

- Read *My dictionary* as a class. Ask pupils to find the sticker and trace the words.
- Ask pupils to read and complete the *What have I learnt?* box individually.

UNIT 2
PAGE 22

Objective:

Pupils will understand the benefits of a healthy diet and the importance of eating five times a day, choosing healthy snacks.

Key vocabulary

breakfast, dinner, healthy, lunch, snack, unhealthy

Warm up

Stick pictures of healthy/unhealthy food around the walls of the classroom. When you say *healthy/unhealthy*, pupils run and touch the correct picture.

Main concepts

- Read the lesson title as a class and discuss pupils' answers.
- Ask pupils what the two labels mean: *healthy snacks* and *unhealthy snacks*. They name the snacks and think of others they know. Then, pupils draw a healthy snack.
- Draw pupils' attention to the *Tip* and ask a volunteer to explain it. Discuss the importance of a balanced diet.
- Read the Fun Fact. Ask for opinions.

Learn more

Create a *Snack chart*. Every day, pupils vote for the person who brought the healthiest snack.

Because our body uses water to function and water contains minerals.

WHY IS WATER GOOD FOR YOU?

Find out

Draw another healthy snack.

healthy snacks

unhealthy snacks

Tip

Eat five times a day and don't forget to drink water!

breakfast

snack

lunch

snack

dinner

FUN FACT

10 sugar cubes = 1 can of cola

Eat five portions of fruit and vegetables every day!

22

Project Step 2

Add more information to your food diary.

1 Add your snack, lunch and dinner to your diary. Draw.

2 Tell your partner.

3 Circle the healthy food in your diary.

Try it out

MY DICTIONARY

breakfast

snack

lunch

dinner

What have I learnt?

It is very healthy to eat five times a day:

1 ______________________

2 ______________________

3 ______________________

4 ______________________

5 ______________________

How much food in your diary is healthy?

23

It is very healthy to eat five times a day: breakfast, snack, lunch, snack, dinner.

UNIT 2
PAGE 23

Objective:

In Step 2 of the project, pupils will reflect on their food habits and whether or not they are healthy.

Key vocabulary

breakfast, dinner, healthy, lunch, snack, unhealthy

Warm up

Using the food pictures, pupils classify them according to which meal it is best to eat them with: breakfast, lunch, dinner or as a snack.

Main concepts

- Look at the instructions together and ask a volunteer to explain.
- Pupils complete their diaries individually, then work in pairs or small groups to show each other.
- Pupils circle all the healthy food in their diaries. How healthy are they?

Learn more

- Read *My dictionary* as a class. Ask pupils to find the sticker and trace the words.
- Ask pupils to read and complete the *What have I learnt?* box individually.
- Ask pupils *Is there anything you will stop eating now because you know it is unhealthy?*

UNIT 2
PAGE 24

Objective:

Pupils will learn more about healthy living: doing sport, sleeping and not spending too much time playing video games or watching TV.

Key vocabulary

fit, healthy, heart, muscles, sleep, sport

Warm up

- Do the Mindful time activity.
- Pupils discuss which sports they do. Ask *Why is doing sport important?*

Main concepts

- As a class, discuss the lesson title. Then, in pairs, pupils tell a classmate about their favourite sport.
- Ask pupils what the statements *Sport keeps you fit and healthy. Your heart and muscles grow strong.* mean.
- Ask *What else can we do to be healthy?* Give them some time to think and respond, then read and discuss *3 Golden Rules*.
- Read the Super-Human Fact.
- Pupils find the hidden basketball.

Learn more

Have a running race in the playground. Pupils see how far they can run in ten seconds. Then they compare with the 100-metre world record.

Yes, it is, because … (accept any suitable answers).

IS WALKING GOOD FOR YOU?

Tell a classmate your favourite sport.

Sport keeps you fit and healthy.
Your heart and muscles grow strong.

3 Golden Rules

30 minutes of sport every day.

Sleep 10 hours a day.

1 hour of TV or video games a day, only.

SUPER-HUMAN FACT

The world record for the 100 metre sprint is 9.58 seconds!

Find the basketball hidden in the unit!

24

It's on page 20, behind the Find out icon.

Game Zone

Try it out

1 Play *Steal the ball.*

1 Get into two groups and line up. Give everyone in each group a number.

2 The teacher places a ball between the teams and calls a number.

3 The first player to take the ball to their team without being tagged is the winner!

2 How do you feel after playing? Tick (✓).

☐ happy ☐ calm ☐ angry ☐ sad

MY DICTIONARY

keep fit

sport

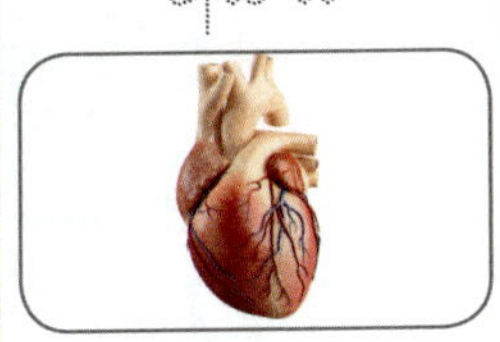

heart

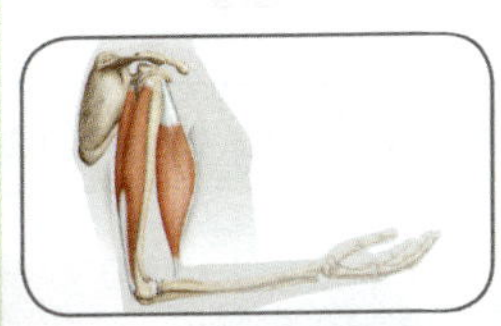

muscles

What have I learnt?

Sport is good for my h__________ and m__________.

It helps me keep f__________.

25

Sport is good for my heart and muscles. It helps me keep fit.

UNIT 2
PAGE 25

Objective:

Pupils will understand the benefits of physical exercise and learn the importance of team work.

Key vocabulary

keep fit, heart, muscles, sport

Warm up

Ask pupils what kind of games they prefer: individual, pair or team games, and why. Ask *What do you play at break times?* Ask them why it is good to be part of a team.

Main concepts

- Read the instructions for *Steal the ball*. Make sure everyone understands the rules, then play the game.
- Ask pupils to complete Activity 2 and share their feelings with a classmate.
- Ask pupils to sit quietly and feel their heartbeats. Then, ask them to jump, hop or run on the spot for a minute. *Now feel your heartbeat again. What is different?*
- Finish with the Mindful time activity.

Learn more

- Read *My dictionary* as a class. Ask pupils to find the sticker and trace the words.
- Ask pupils to read and complete the *What have I learnt?* box individually.

UNIT 2
PAGE 26

Objective:

Pupils will learn about healthy habits related to personal hygiene.

Key vocabulary

brush, hands, shower, teeth, wash

Warm up

Check pupils understand the difference between *clean* and *dirty*. Start a discussion about the importance of keeping ourselves clean and the consequences of not doing so. Ask for examples of how we can keep ourselves clean.

Main concepts

- Read the lesson title with the class. Give them time to think, then elicit responses. Ask *How many times a day do you brush your teeth?*
- Ask pupils to read the advice on the page. Ask *Do you do these things? Do you think they are important to do?*
- As a class, read the question *Who is doing the right thing?* Ask pupils to look at the photos in pairs, think and tick a box. Discuss the answer.

Learn more

In their notebooks or on card, pupils can draw a picture of themselves and use speech bubbles to give advice about how to keep clean.

Pupils' own answers – ideally, should be at least 2 minutes

HOW LONG DO YOU BRUSH YOUR TEETH FOR?

Find out

Who is doing the right thing? Tick (✓).

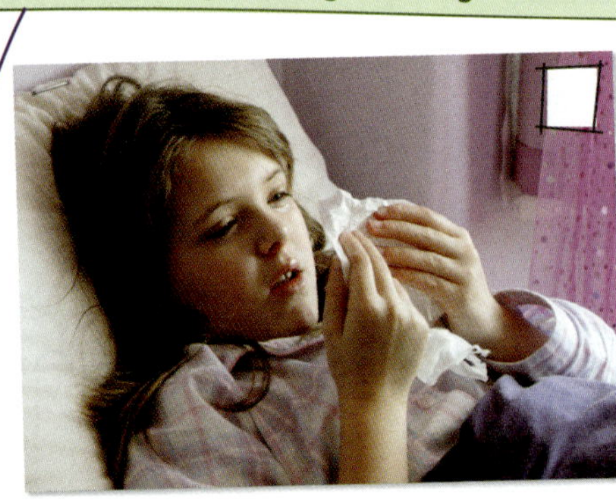

26

The girl because she is in bed and she is using a tissue.

Experiment

Find out what cola, vinegar and water do to eggs.

1 Put an egg in cola. Observe it for **a day**.

2 Put another egg in **vinegar**. Observe it for **two days**.

3 Put a third egg in **water**. Observe it for **three days**.

What happens to egg number 1?

What happens to egg number 2?

What happens to egg number 3?

Conclusion

Which egg changed first?

1 2 3

Which egg stayed healthy?

1 2 3

What happens if you do not brush your teeth?

Objective:

Pupils will learn about the importance of water for their bodies, and dental hygiene.

Key vocabulary

brush, cola, eggs, teeth, vinegar, water

Warm up

Show pupils the objects they are going to use for the experiment. Ask *What are we going to do?* Encourage pupils to be imaginative.

Main concepts

- As a class, read and follow out the instructions 1–3.
- Ask pupils to work in pairs and write in their notebooks what they think will happen to the eggs.
- This process will take a few days, so put the bowls in a safe place in the classroom where they can be observed. After the allotted time, remove the eggs from the liquid. Pupils look back at their predictions and compare with the results. They record their conclusions.

Learn more

You can ask pupils to do the same experiment at home but with a chicken bone, so they can observe what cola, vinegar and water do to our bones. They share their results in class.

UNIT 2
PAGE 28

Objective:

Pupils will think about their own feelings and those of others.

Key vocabulary

angry, calm, happy, sad, worried

Warm up

Have five pieces of paper, each with a key vocabulary word. Check that everyone knows the words. Ask a pupil to take a card and mime the word. The others guess the feeling.

Main concepts

- Pupils work with a classmate. They should tell each other when they feel sad, happy, etc. Give an example, e.g. *I feel happy when it is sunny.*
- Discuss what pupils can see in the photos in Activity 2. Play the audio twice. Let pupils check in pairs. Then check answers together.
- Ask pupils to close their eyes and think about how they feel today. They complete Activity 3.

Learn more

Get pupils to ask family members how they are feeling. They can draw a picture or write it in their notebooks and share with a classmate.

Attitude is everything

1 When do you feel ...?

Pupils' own answers

happy

calm

sad

worried

angry

2 How does Lucy feel? Listen and tick (✓).

happy

3 How do you feel today? Draw and colour.

Pupils' own answers

28

Pupils' own answers – check the food is in the correct group

Now I know

Assessment link
Go to page 80 for more activities.

1 Draw one more item in each section of the food wheel. Colour.

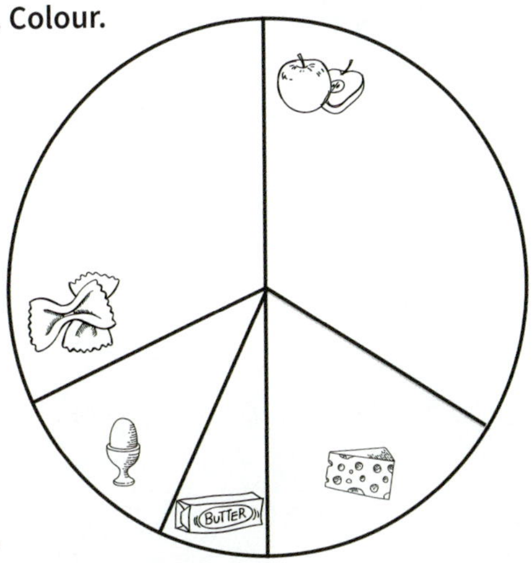

2 Circle the healthy habits.

3 Look at the pictures. Look at the letters. Write the words.

_ _ _ _ _ ruift

_ _ _ _ _ tspor

Chant
Be healthy

I am Louis Pasteur.
I developed the first vaccinations, to stop people from getting sick.

29

Pictures 1 and 3

fruit, sport
This activity gives pupils practice of *Pre-A1 Starters* Reading and Writing Part 3.

UNIT 2
PAGE 29

Objective:

Pupils will review the content of the unit and read about Louis Pasteur.

Key vocabulary

Food groups, healthy and unhealthy habits

Warm up

Sing the chant and the song from the unit. Ask pupils to stand up and do the actions together.

Main concepts

- As a class, read the instructions for Activities 1, 2 and 3. Check comprehension by asking volunteers to say what they have to do for each activity. Pupils complete the tasks in pairs. When everyone has finished, put two pairs together to compare answers. Then, check answers with the whole class.
- As a class, look at the photo of Louis Pasteur and read the information. Explain as needed.

Learn more

- Use the internet to look for more information about Louis Pasteur.
- Go to page 80 for more activities.
- Pupils can now put their fingerprint in the passport on page 5.

UNIT 2 LET'S REVIEW PAGE 80

Find the right words answers

1

a yes

b yes

c no

d no

This activity gives pupils practice of *Pre-A1 Starters* Reading and Writing Part 2.

2

a under

b on

c in

d on

Look back answers

1

1 a banana

2 c crisps

3 c five

This activity gives pupils practice of *Pre-A1 Starters* Listening Part 3.

2

a teeth

b hands

c shower

d TV

e ten

UNIT 2 TRACKLIST

Track 12 Page 19, Song *I like healthy food!*

Track 13 Page 20, *Are all vegetables green?*

Track 14 Page 22, *Why is water good for you?*

Track 15 Page 24, *Is walking good for you?*

Track 16 Page 26, *How long do you brush your teeth for?*

Track 17 Page 28, Listening activity

Track 18 Page 29, Chant *Be Healthy*

Track 19 Page 29, *I am Louis Pasteur.* Character

Track 55 Page 81, Listening activity

Track 59 Page 90, *Story 1. Listen and read.*

Story 1

Topic: Healthy habits and safety

Summary: Little Pasteur and Little Franklin are at the hospital after Little Franklin's birthday party. Little Pasteur has a stomach ache because he ate too much during the party. Little Franklin has a broken arm because she didn't play safely. Both decide to change their habits in the future. When Little Darwin goes to visit with some sweets, Little Pasteur rejects them and he eats an apple instead: he has learned his lesson.

Pupils listen to the story and complete *Now I know* activities on pages 90 and 91

***Now I know* story answers**

1 1, 3, 2

2 She broke her arm.

3

ANIMAL PLANET

Learning objectives

By the end of this unit, your pupils will have achieved a greater understanding of the following concepts:

- the main characteristics and differences between vertebrates and invertebrates
- how different animals move
- the five vertebrate groups: mammal, bird, fish, reptile and amphibian
- the differences between wild and domestic animals

Competences

This unit covers the following competences:

- Linguistic competence
- Mathematical competence and basic competences in science and technology
- Digital competence
- Learning to learn
- Social and civic competences
- Cultural awareness and expression

Key vocabulary

Animal characteristics: domestic, invertebrates, vertebrates, wild

Animal habitats: Arctic, farm, ocean, rainforest

Animal movement: fly, slither, swim, walk

Animal groups: amphibians, birds, fish, mammals, reptiles

Cambridge English Qualifications practice

You will find *Pre-A1 Starters* activity types in the following exercises:

Pupil's Book, Page 83, Activity 2 – Listening Part 4

Activity Book, Page 15, Activity 3 – Reading and Writing Part 1

Activity Book, Page 17, Activity 7 – Reading and Writing Part 3

Activity Book, Page 19, Activity 11 – Reading and Writing Part 4

Throughout this unit, you will find the following *Pre-A1 Starters* vocabulary:

animal, baby, balloon, bat, bear, bird, can, cat, cow, dog, eat, find, fish, fly, have (got), horse, learn, like, look, make, monkey, pet, play, point, polar bear, sad, snake, swim, tiger, walk

Materials needed for *project*:

- Cotton, crayons, glue sticks, paper, scissors, shoe boxes

Materials needed for *experiment*:

- Breadcrumbs, cereal, corn, glue, lolly sticks, milk cartons, plastic cups, scissors, seeds, string

Experiment

The *experiment* provides your pupils with the opportunity to care for wildlife and the environment. They will discover what kinds of food birds prefer. In addition, this will be their first experiment outdoors and they will observe the different factors that can affect the results, such as weather conditions and the influence of other humans or animals.

Mindful time

Each unit has a mindful time feature that encourages pupils to relate learning to their feelings and emotions, their relationships with classmates, and their well-being.

In this unit, pupils learn to focus their attention by listening to an audio track *(track 20)* with sounds of different animals and nature.

Digital Lab +

- Interactive activities
- Flashcards: animals
- Song: *Move like an animal*
- Chant: *Wild, domestic*
- Video documentary: *Animal trip*

UNIT 3
PAGES 30–31

Objective:

The opening spread will introduce pupils to different types of animals and some of their characteristics. Pupils will think about and use concepts they have learned in previous units. They will also consider different feelings and emotions.

Key vocabulary

fly, frog, hop, horse, jump, rabbit, run, sad, sheep, snake

Warm up

Ask pupils to look at the picture on pages 30–31. Get them to guess where the characters are – in a forest. *What animals can you see? – I can see … Do you know any other animals that live in the forest?*

Main concepts

- Ask a pupil to read the title of the unit. Ask the class *What is this unit about? – Animals!*
- Ask pupils to think about the animals they know. *Do they all look the same? Do they move in the same way? Do they eat the same food? Can you keep them all at home?*
- Draw pupils' attention back to the page, ask *Who is sad? Why do you think they are sad?* Give pupils time to study the characters before taking answers

Pupils' own answers (accept any appropriate answer)

a fly, frog, horse, rabbit, sheep and snake

Mindful time

Pupils will listen to sounds of nature. They will close their eyes and focus their attention on the animal and environmental sounds they hear.

Little Curie and Little Pasteur

Because Little Darwin is leaving (to learn about animals).

Learn more

- Do the Mindful time: ask pupils to identify the sounds they hear.
- Display pictures of animals you can find in different environments. Write some environment names on the board, e.g. ocean, desert, etc. Ask pupils to match the animals to the correct environment.

Song

The song focuses on how different animals move.

Documentary

The documentary focuses on the different types and classes of animals and their habitats.

UNIT 3
PAGE 32

Objective:

Pupils will understand the difference between vertebrates and invertebrates.

Key vocabulary

balloon fish, invertebrate, jellyfish, skeleton, vertebrate

Warm up

Ask pupils to draw a fish. In groups, they discuss the similarities and differences of their fish.

Main concepts

- Draw pupils' attention to the photos and information on the page. Ask them to look and read. Then ask for volunteers to tell the class what they have learnt. Clarify the differences between a vertebrate and an invertebrate.
- Read the questions in the bubbles together and discuss.
- Pupils draw a vertebrate. Allow them to ask you for ideas or to do research.
- Read the Fun Fact.

Learn more

Pupils find out if the electric eel is a vertebrate or invertebrate. They can also research more vertebrate and invertebrate animals.

No, they aren't. Some are vertebrate and some are invertebrate.

Because it looks like jelly – soft and wobbly.

Because it blows up and is round like a balloon.

Project Step 1

Try it out

Let's explore the ocean!

1 Find a shoe box. Draw an ocean background.

2 Draw, colour and stick the animals in the ocean.

Point to the vertebrates and invertebrates.

MY DICTIONARY

balloon fish

crab

invertebrate

vertebrate

What have I learnt?

A ______________ has got a skeleton.
An ______________ has not got a skeleton.
A ______________ is an invertebrate.
A ______________ ______________ is a vertebrate.

33

A vertebrate has got a skeleton. An invertebrate hasn't got a skeleton. A crab is an invertebrate. A balloon fish is a vertebrate.

UNIT 3
PAGE 33

Objective:

Pupils will consolidate their understanding of vertebrates and invertebrates. They will create an ocean box.

Key vocabulary

balloon fish, crab, invertebrate, vertebrate

Warm up

Show pupils photos of different sea creatures and ask pupils which is the animals' normal habitat – the ocean/sea.

Main concepts

- Play the documentary *Animal trip*.
- Say *Let's explore the ocean!* Go through the instructions with pupils. Pupils complete the task using a variety of vertebrate and invertebrate sea animals.
- Encourage pupils to tell a classmate about the vertebrates and invertebrates in their ocean.

Learn more

- Read *My dictionary* as a class. Ask pupils to find the sticker and trace the words.
- Ask pupils to read and complete the *What have I learnt?* box individually.

UNIT 3
PAGE 34

Objective:

Pupils will investigate and learn four ways in which animals can move.

Key vocabulary

fish, fly, fur, polar bear, puffin, seal, slither, swim, transparent, walk

Warm up

Play a game. Pretend you are a bird and you are flying around the class. Ask pupils *What am I? – a bird/bat*, etc. *What am I doing? How do I move? – You're flying. / You fly.* Pupils can take turns pretending they are different animals, moving in different ways.

Main concepts

- Ask pupils to look at the photos and read the words. Can they identify the animals? (puffin, polar bear, seal, fish) Ask them to be each animal, e.g. a flying puffin. Then, ask them what body parts each animal uses to move.
- As a class, read the Fun Fact and discuss the question in the bubble.
- Pupils colour the jumping fish.

Learn more

Either show pupils a video of jumping fish and polar bears swimming or help them to do research and find them themselves. Tell them to find out how the fish jump.

Yes, they can.

Because it reflects the snow.

UNIT 3
PAGE 35

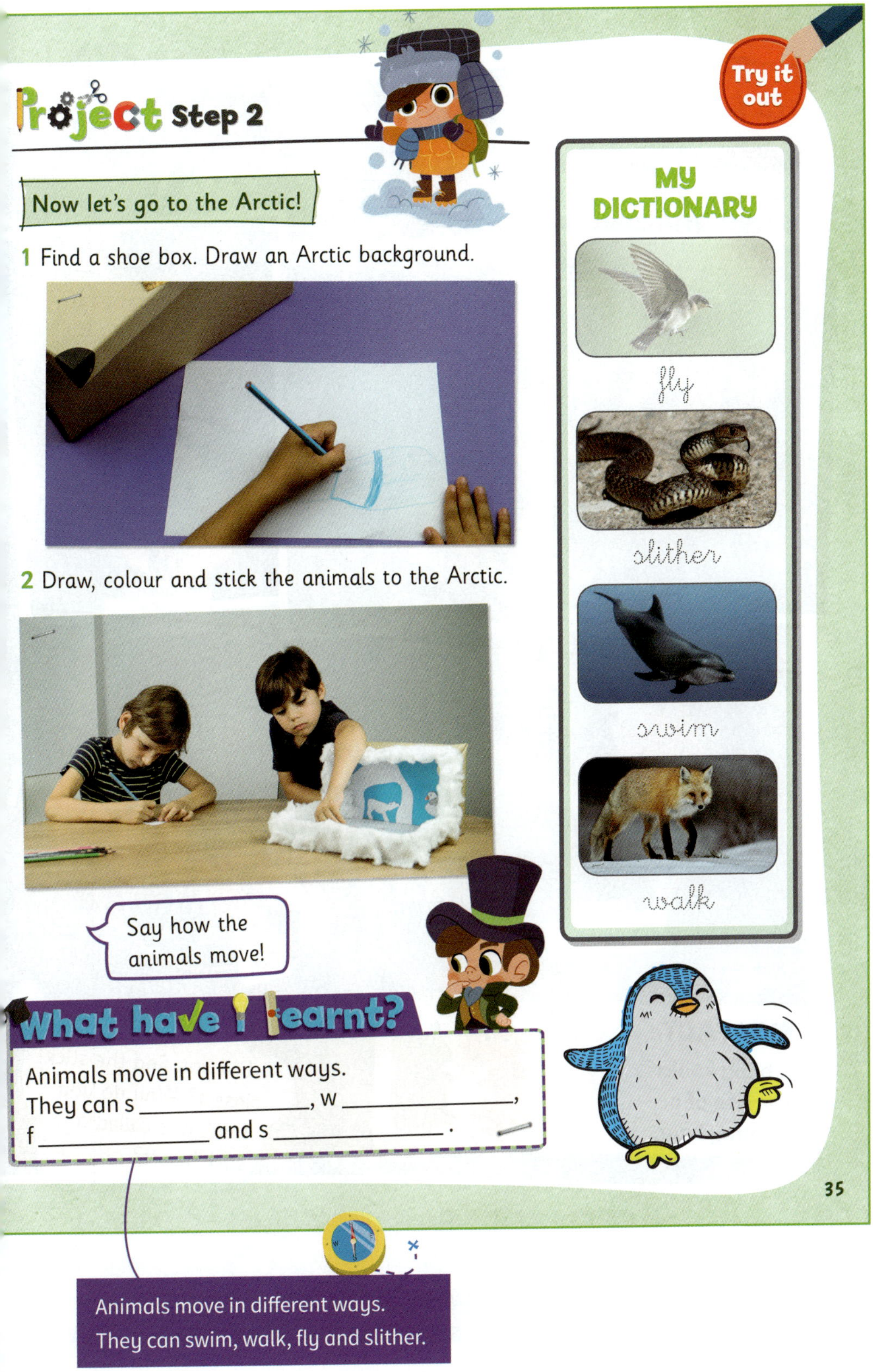

Project Step 2

Now let's go to the Arctic!

1 Find a shoe box. Draw an Arctic background.

2 Draw, colour and stick the animals to the Arctic.

Try it out

MY DICTIONARY

fly

slither

swim

walk

Say how the animals move!

What have I learnt?

Animals move in different ways.
They can s ____________, w ____________,
f ____________ and s ____________.

35

Animals move in different ways.
They can swim, walk, fly and slither.

Objective:

Pupils will consolidate their understanding of how animals move. They will create an Arctic box.

Key vocabulary

fly, slither, swim, walk

Tip

Play the documentary *Animal trip* and draw pupils' attention to the Arctic animals.

Warm up

Show the pupils flashcards of different animals and ask them how they move. Ask them which animals live in the Arctic.

Main concepts

- Say *Let's go to the Arctic!* Go through the instructions as a class. Point out that this time pupils should choose animals that live in the Arctic. Pupils complete the task.
- Encourage pupils to show and talk about their Arctic box to a classmate.

Learn more

- Read *My dictionary* as a class. Ask pupils to find the sticker and trace the words.
- Ask pupils to read and complete the *What have I learnt?* box individually.•

UNIT 3
PAGE 36

Objective:

Pupils will learn about amphibians, birds, fish, mammals and reptiles, and their characteristics.

Key vocabulary

amphibian, bird, fish, koala, mammal, stick insect, reptile

Warm up

Show pupils pictures of animals from each group and elicit some of their characteristics, e.g. *Snakes haven't got legs. They slither. Birds have got wings. They fly.*, etc. Write some examples on the board.

Main concepts

- Ask pupils to look at the photos and labels on the page. Can they add the animals from the Warm up to the correct group? Discuss the characteristics of each group.
- Ask pupils *Is a bat a bird?* Discuss their ideas.
- Pupils find the stick insect. Read the speech bubble together and discuss.
- Read the Fun Fact.

Learn more

Present one animal from each group that the pupils haven't seen in the lesson. In groups, pupils discuss and decide which group the animal belongs to.

No, it isn't. The bat is a mammal. It hasn't got a beak and it hasn't got feathers.

IS A BAT A BIRD?

Find out

Find and circle the stick insect.

FUN FACT
A baby koala is the size of a gummy bear!

Did you find the stick insect? Why do you think it is called a stick insect?

36

Because it looks like a stick to camouflage itself.

Project Step 3

Let's finish our adventure in the rainforest.

Try it out

1 Find a shoe box. Draw a forest background.

2 Draw, colour and stick the animals to the forest.

Say how the animals move!

What have I learnt?

There are five types of vertebrate:

amphibians ___________ ___________

___________ ___________

____

Display your adventures in your classroom!

My dictionary

amphibians

birds

fish

mammals

reptiles

37

There are five types of vertebrate: amphibians, birds, fish, mammals, reptiles. (any order)

UNIT 3
PAGE 37

Objective:

Pupils will consolidate their understanding of the animal groups, and make a rainforest box.

Key vocabulary

amphibians, birds, fish, mammals, reptiles, vertebrate

Warm up

Show pupils photos of different animals that live in the rainforest. Say *How do they move? What sounds do they make?* Encourage pupils to act it out.

Main concepts

- Go through the instructions with pupils, reminding them that this time the animals should live in the rainforest. Pupils complete the task.
- Do the Mindful time: tell pupils to breathe deeply and relax to the sounds. Can they identify any rainforest sounds?
- Pupils choose a box: rainforest, Arctic or ocean, and present it to the class. You could ask them to prepare it at home and present in the next lesson.

Learn more

- Read *My dictionary* as a class. Ask pupils to find the sticker and trace the words.
- Ask pupils to read and complete the *What have I learnt?* box individually.

UNIT 3
PAGE 38

Objective:

Pupils will be able to identify and classify wild and domestic animals.

Key vocabulary

badger, chick, cow, domestic, fox, hen, horse, sheep, owl, pet, wild

Warm up

Sing the nursery rhyme *Old MacDonald*. Have pupils do animal mimes and make the noises. Then ask pupils to name the animals. Write them on the board.

Main concepts

- Read the title question with pupils. Give them time to think and answer. Ask *Why? / Why not?*
- Ask *What's your favourite animal on the page? Can it live with us at home?* Explain that pets and farm animals are domestic and that other animals are wild. Get pupils to identify which animals are domestic and which are wild.
- Read the instruction with the class. Play the audio twice. Let pupils compare answers before confirming.

Learn more

- Read the Fun Fact. Explain as necessary.
- Do the chant: *Wild, domestic.*

No, they aren't.

Experiment

Try it out

Find out what birds eat.

1 Cut some windows in a milk carton. Make two holes near the bottom and put a stick through them.

2 Fill the carton with different food: breadcrumbs, corn, cereal and seeds.

3 Hang the carton outside and observe.

Predict

Which food do you think the birds will like the most?

Pupils' own answers

You can also paint and decorate your milk carton.

Conclusion

What is the birds' favourite food?

Was your prediction correct?

Pupils' own answers

39

Objective:

Pupils will perform an experiment to find out what type of food birds prefer.

Key vocabulary

breadcrumbs, cereal, corn, milk carton, seeds, stick, predict

Warm up

Show pupils pictures of different types of food, e.g. fruit, meat, cheese, seeds, etc. Say *Do you know what birds eat? Do you think birds will like these types of food?*

Main concepts

- Say *We're going to find out what birds eat*. Go through the instructions, explaining as necessary. Pupils build their bird feeders.
- Ask pupils to make and record their prediction, then hang their feeders in a green area.
- After a day or two, pupils should revisit the bird feeder and complete the conclusion. How many pupils predicted correctly?

Learn more

Pupils take their bird feeders home and fill them with other types of food to see what food birds in their neighbourhood prefer. They should be careful not to use anything which may be harmful to birds.

UNIT 3
PAGE 40

Objective:

Pupils will practise animal yoga postures and think about animal welfare.

Key vocabulary

abandon, butterfly, cat, cow, dog, feed, monkey, play, snake, wash

Warm up

Do the Mindful time activity from Unit 1: Belly breathing.

Main concepts

- Demonstrate the yoga positions in the book. You should do each very slowly and hold the position for a few seconds. Pupils do the same.
- Ask *How do you feel? Which part of the butterfly were your legs? – The wings.*, etc.
- Ask if anyone has a pet. *What have you got? How do you take care of him/her?* Emphasise the need to treat and take care of all animals well. Try to create a responsible attitude and stress the importance of never abandoning your pet. Pupils complete the task.

Learn more

Encourage pupils to share ideas about how they can look after their pets responsibly. *How can you help other animals? – Put food out for wild birds.*, etc.

Pupils' own answers

Attitude is everything

1 Do animal yoga with your teacher. Which animal is your favourite?

2 Look after pets. Match the sentences to the correct picture.

Feed your pet. | Wash your pet. | Play with your pet.

Never abandon your pet!

UNIT 3
PAGE 41

b, c, e

Now I know

Assessment link
Go to page 82 for more activities.

1 Listen and circle the invertebrates.

a

b

c

d

e

f

2 Can you remember? Classify the animals.

cat fox hen badger tiger horse

domestic animals	wild animals

domestic animals: cat, hen, horse
wild animals: fox, badger, tiger

Chant
Wild, domestic

I am Charles Darwin.
I studied animals all over the world.

41

Objective:
Pupils will review the content of the unit and read about Charles Darwin.

Key vocabulary
badger, butterfly, cat, cow, crab, dog, fox, hen, horse, jellyfish, snake, tiger

Warm up
Sing and do actions to the chant *Wild, domestic*.

Main concepts
- Elicit what an invertebrate is, then read the instructions together for Activity 1. Play the audio twice, pausing when necessary. Allow pupils to compare with a classmate before checking answers.
- Have pupils complete Activity 2 in pairs. Then they compare answers with another pair.
- Look at the photo of Charles Darwin and read the information.

Learn more
- Get pupils to find out about some animals discovered by Charles Darwin.
- Go to page 82 for more activities.
- Pupils can now put their fingerprint in the passport on page 5.

UNIT 3 LET'S REVIEW PAGE 82

Find the right words answers

1

a Yes, it is.

b No, it isn't.

c No, it isn't.

2

a I haven't got a skeleton.

b I have got a skeleton.

Look back answers

1

a slither

b swim

c fly

d slither

e walk

f fly

2

Fox: orange

Bird: brown

Fish: purple

Trees: green

This activity gives pupils practice of *Pre-A1 Starters* Listening Part 4.

UNIT 3 TRACKLIST

Track 20 Page 30, Mindful time. *Sounds of nature*
Track 21 Page 31, Song *Move like an animal*
Track 22 Page 32, *Are all fish the same?*
Track 23 Page 34, *Can polar bears swim?*
Track 24 Page 36, *Is a bat a bird?*
Track 25 Page 38, *Are all animals good pets?*
Track 26 Page 38, Listening activity
Track 27 Page 41, Listening activity
Track 28 Page 41, Chant *Wild, domestic*
Track 29 Page 41, *I am Charles Darwin*. Character
Track 56 Page 83, Listening activity

4

FLOWER POWER!

Learning objectives

By the end of this unit, your pupils will have achieved a greater understanding of the following concepts:

- the main parts of a plant
- different types of plant: grass, bush and tree
- plant classification: wild and cultivated
- plant usage

Competences

This unit covers the following competences:

- Linguistic competence
- Mathematical competence and basic competences in science and technology
- Digital competence
- Learning to learn
- Social and civic competences
- Cultural awareness and expression

Key vocabulary

Plant parts: flower, leaf, root, seed, stem

Types of plants and their characteristics: branch, bendy, bush, grass, stem, thick, tree, trunk, wheat, woody

Plant classification: algae, chamomile, cotton, cultivated, dandelion, farmer, field, pine, strawberry, thistle, wild

Plant usage: chair, clothes, cotton, food, furniture, jam, medicine, pine tree, table, t-shirt, tea

Cambridge English Qualifications practice

You will find *Pre-A1 Starters* activity types in the following exercises:

Pupil's Book, Page 53, Activity 1 – Listening Part 1

Pupil's Book, Page 85, Activity 2 – Reading and Writing Part 3

Activity Book, Page 21, Activity 3 – Reading and Writing Part 1

Activity Book, Page 21, Activity 4 – Reading and Writing Part 4

Activity Book, Page 22, Activity 6 – Reading and Writing Part 2

Throughout this unit, you will find the following *Pre-A1 Starters* vocabulary:

add, baby, bag, be, bean, close, come, do, draw, drink, eat, face, flower, happy, have, know, listen, name, new, onion, page, put, sad, sun, tick, tree, water, window, write

Materials needed for *project*:

- A piece of cloth, seeds (beans, chickpeas or lentils), a Ziploc type bag; cola, vinegar, water; a drawer; a plastic container, soil

Project

The project runs through the unit and provides pupils with the opportunity to germinate seeds. Pupils will experiment with seeds and see how they develop using different types of liquid, a lack of air and a lack of sunlight.

Mindful time

Each unit has a mindful time feature that encourages pupils to relate learning to their feelings and emotions, their relationships with classmates, and their well-being.

In this unit, pupils breathe like a tree and learn to connect and identify their feelings while breathing.

Digital Lab +

Interactive activities

Flashcards: plants

Song: *I am a plant*

Chant: *Plants are useful*

Video documentary: *All about plants*

UNIT 4
PAGES 42–43

Objective:

The opening spread will provide pupils with the opportunity to consider different types of plants and to explore some of their characteristics and what they need to survive. They will think about and put into use concepts from earlier units.

Key vocabulary

flowers, live, okay, plants, trees, worry, worried

Warm up

- Ask pupils to look at the picture on pages 42–43. Ask *Where are the characters?* Accept all appropriate answers. *Can you remember the character's names?*
- Say *What can you see in the garden? – I can see … plants/flowers/trees!*

Main concepts

- Ask a pupil to read the title of the unit. Say *What is this unit about? – Flowers/Plants.*
- Ask pupils to think about any plants they know. *Do they all look the same? How can we care for them? Are they useful or just an ornament? Do you have a favourite plant or flower?* Elicit responses and help with vocabulary.
- Focus on the questions. Ask pupils to explain what is happening. Elicit what plants need to survive.

No, it is wilting/dying.

Mindful time

Pupils will stand, close their eyes, put their arms out like the branches of a tree and gently sway in the wind. They will focus on relaxed, even breathing and how they are feeling.

air, earth, sunlight and water

She is worried/sad.

Learn more

As a class, ask pupils if they can think of any plants that we eat. Elicit responses and encourage discussion.

Song
The song focuses on plant parts and their functions.

Documentary
The documentary focuses on the different types of plants, their features, where they can be found and their usage.

UNIT 4
PAGE 44

Objective:

Pupils will learn the parts of a plant and recognise that some are edible.

Key vocabulary

asparagus, cauliflower, flower, leaves, lettuce, onion, roots, stem

Warm up

Show pupils pictures of different edible plants and ask them to identify which is the edible part. They don't need to produce the vocabulary, just point.

Main concepts

- Go through the information in the speech bubbles with pupils. Ask them whether they eat these vegetables and whether they like them.
- As a class, read the instructions. Play the audio. Check that pupils understand how each vegetable relates to the parts of the plant.
- Read the Fun Fact and discuss why onions make you cry – they release an irritant when you cut them and your tears help wash it away.

Learn more

Ask pupils to bring in pictures of plants we can eat. Make a poster classifying the plants depending on their edible part.

Yes, we eat some flowers like cauliflower and broccoli.

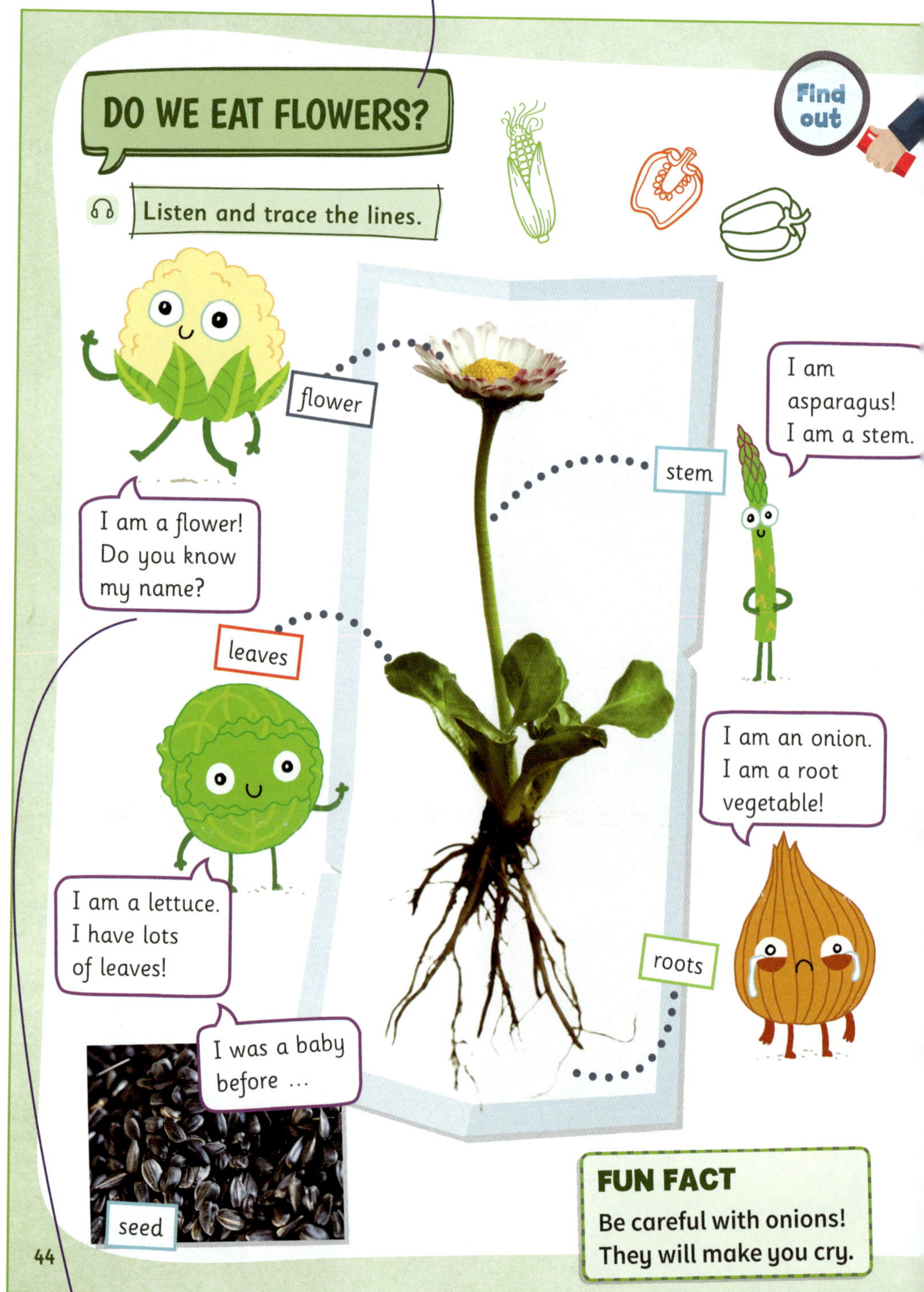

Cauliflower.

Project Step 1

What's in the box?

1 Seeds! Let's germinate them!
Wet a cloth with water. Put some seeds in the cloth. Place the cloth in a bag and seal it.

2 Everyone in the class hangs their bag next to a window.

Predict

What do you think will happen?

Try it out

MY DICTIONARY

What have I learnt?

Plants have got f_______________, l_______________, r_______________ and a s_______________.
Some plants grow from s_______________.

45

Plants have got flowers, leaves, roots and a stem. Some plants grow from seeds.

UNIT 4
PAGE 45

Objective:

Pupils will learn how to germinate a seed. They will make a scientific prediction.

Key vocabulary

bag, cloth, flowers, leaves, roots, seeds, stem

Warm up

- Sing *I am a plant*.
- Show pupils the box and encourage them to guess what's inside it – seeds. You can shake it to give the pupils a clue.

Main concepts

- Ask pupils to open their books and take a look at the project. Say *We are going to germinate some seeds!*
- Go through the instructions with pupils. Explain that they should be careful and not add too much water. Pupils complete the task.
- Ask them to predict what will happen to the seeds. Make a record of their predictions, e.g. in a class chart, in their notebooks, etc.

Learn more

- Read *My dictionary* as a class. Ask pupils to find the sticker and trace the words.
- Ask pupils to read and complete the *What have I learnt?* box individually.

UNIT 4
PAGE 46

Objective:

Pupils will learn about three types of plant: bushes, grass and trees, and their main parts.

Key vocabulary

bendy, branch, bush, grass, stem, thick, trunk, woody

Warm up

Do the Mindful time and extend by asking pupils to *crouch like a bush* (crouched down in a ball), and *sway like grass* (standing with arms straight up, above the head, and sway).

Main concepts

- Ask pupils to look at the photos and labels. Point out, stem, branch and trunk, and elicit the differences. Ask *Is grass always green?* If necessary, draw pupils' attention to the wheat.
- Say *What food can you see?* (apples, blackberries and wheat) Pupils may not see wheat as food, so discuss with them how wheat can be used, e.g. flour for bread/biscuits, etc.
- Read the Fun Fact. Explain as necessary and ask pupils how they feel about that fact.

Learn more

Pupils find out what different food items at home contain wheat and report their findings in the next class.

Project Step 2

What do plants drink?

1 Work in groups. Take three plants from the line. Add cola to one of the plants. Add vinegar to another one.

2 Add water to the third Let's call this plant *Control plant* – write it on the bag.

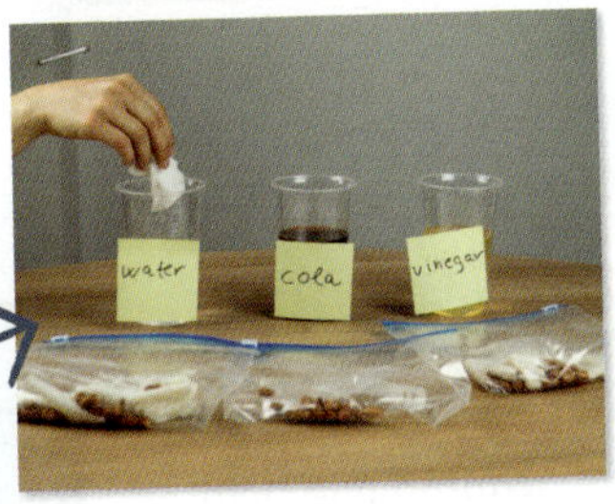

Try it out

Predict

What will happen to the plants?

Control plant

Hang the bags up again. Make sure they are closed.

MY DICTIONARY

bush

grass

tree

trunk

woody stems

What have I learnt?

Trees have got a t_______________ .
Bushes have got lots of w_______________
s_______________ .
G_______________ is bendy.

47

Trees have got a trunk. Bushes have got lots of woody stems. Grass is bendy.

UNIT 4
PAGE 47

Objective:

Pupils will discover that plants need water to survive.

Key vocabulary

bush, cola, control, grass, tree, trunk, vinegar, water, woody stems

Warm up

Ask *What do you think plants drink?* Do you think they like cola and vinegar? Accept all answers, but don't confirm at this point. *Let's find out!*

Main concepts

- Ask pupils about any changes that may have happened to the plants since they were first hung.
- Guide pupils through Project Step 2. Make sure they close the bags properly.
- Ask pupils to predict what will happen to the plants. Predictions should be added to the record.

Learn more

- Read *My dictionary* as a class. Ask pupils to find the sticker and trace the words.
- Ask pupils to read and complete the *What have I learnt?* box individually

UNIT 4
PAGE 48

Objective:

Pupils will learn that there are wild and cultivated plants.

Key vocabulary

algae, chamomile, cotton, cultivated, dandelion, farmer, field, pine, strawberry, thistle, wild

Warm up

Display a picture of a field of wild flowers next to a field of cultivated flowers. Ask pupils which flowers they prefer and why. Explain one is grown and cared for to be sold or used, and the other grows freely and sometimes considered a weed. *What do you think about this?*

Main concepts

- Discuss the title question.
- Look at the cultivated plants on the page and ask pupils what each plant could be used for.
- Repeat with the wild plants. Then ask pupils the activity question. Give them time to think and formulate their answers.
- Do Mindful time: pupils imagine they are a wild flower, then a cultivated flower. *Do you feel different?*

Learn more

- Read and answer the bubble question together.
- Read the Fun Fact.

No, some plants grow wild.

Suggested answers: potatoes, lettuce, tomatoes, fruit trees, etc. They also work with animals.

Objective:
Pupils will learn the importance of sunlight and air for plants.

Key vocabulary

cotton, cultivated, drawer, farmer, fields, wild

Project Step 3

Try it out

Do plants need sunlight?

1 Work in your groups. Take a new bag from the line. Put it in a drawer.

2 Observe the new plant and the *Control* plant. What happens to each plant?

My Dictionary

cotton

cultivated

farmer

fields

wild

What have I learnt?

W_____________ plants grow everywhere.
A farmer grows c_____________ plants in f_____________.
C_____________ is a cultivated plant.

Wild plants grow everywhere. A farmer grows cultivated plants in fields. Cotton is a cultivated plant.

49

Warm up

Display photos of healthy plants in an appropriate setting e.g. windowsill, and unhealthy/dying plants in a shady/dark place, e.g. in a cupboard/corner of a room. Point out the unhealthy plants, say *What do you think is wrong with these plants?*

Main concepts

- Elicit what pupils can remember from Steps 1 and 2.
- Go through the instructions with pupils. They complete the task.
- Ask pupils to make predictions about what will happen to the plants. Add their predictions to the record.
- Pupils check the plants in a few days to see what has happened.

Learn more

- Read *My dictionary* as a class. Ask pupils to find the sticker and trace the words.
- Ask pupils to read and complete the *What have I learnt?* box individually.
- Sing *I am a plant*.

UNIT 4
PAGE 50

Objective:

Pupils will learn about the ways plants can be used and the useful things they provide us with.

Key vocabulary

chair, clothes, cotton, food, furniture, (strawberry) jam, medicine, pine tree, table, (chamomile) tea, t-shirt

Warm up

Display photos of everyday objects made from plants, e.g. books, jam, a cotton t-shirt, a wooden window frame, etc. Ask pupils *What are these things made of? Where does it come from?*

Main concepts

- Pupils point to the things they use every day. Ask them what they are called and elicit the generic nouns: *food, furniture, clothes, medicine.*
- In small groups, ask pupils to think of one or two more examples of *food, furniture, clothes* and *medicine* made from plants.
- Elicit from pupils what a sunflower is. Ask them to find the sunflower hidden in the unit.

Learn more

Give each pupil the name of a plant. They find out what that plant provides for us. They can make a list with words or drawings.

Paper comes from trees.

It's next to the title on page 48.

1 😃 = water.
😭 = cola or vinegar. Plants need *water*.

2 😭 = cupboard.
😃 = window. Plants need *sunlight*.

Project Step 4

Try it out

What do plants need? Circle the correct face.

1 😃 😭 water
😃 😭 cola or vinegar

Plants need w______________ .

2 😃 😭 cupboard
😃 😭 window

Plants need s_______light.

Plants also need **air**.

Take your *Control plant* out of the bag and put it in soil, inside a plastic container. You will need it for the next unit!

MY DICTIONARY

clothes

food

furniture

medicine

What have I learnt?

We use plants to make c______________ ,
fu______________ , m______________ ,
and f______________ .

We use plants to make clothes, furniture, medicine and food.

UNIT 4
PAGE 51

Objective:

Pupils will reflect on what they have learnt from the project and record their conclusions.

Key vocabulary

clothes, cupboard, food, furniture, medicine, plastic container, soil, window

Warm up

Ask pupils to tell you what they did and what they discovered during Steps 1–3 of the project.

Main concepts

- As a class, read the activity rubric. Give pupils time to complete the task.
- Draw pupils' attention to the text: *Plants also need air.*
- Read the instructions and help pupils to complete the task. Store the container in a visible place in the classroom.

Learn more

- Read *My dictionary* as a class. Ask pupils to find the sticker and trace the words.
- Ask pupils to read and complete the *What have I learnt?* box individually.

UNIT 4
PAGE 52

Objective:

Pupils will consolidate their knowledge of plant care and review vocabulary.

Key vocabulary

calm, cupboard, fresh, happy, pick, sad, step on, water, wild, worried

Warm up

Do the Mindful time activity, include the bush and grass movements.

Main concepts

- Begin with books closed. Ask pupils what they can remember about taking care of plants.
- Read the Activity 1 instruction together. Read through the options and help with vocabulary. Pupils complete the task.
- Say *Remember the Mindful time activity. How do you feel when you breathe like a tree?* Pupils circle the word that describes how they feel and draw their face.

Learn more

Encourage pupils to practise a responsible attitude towards plants. They could go on plant patrol and help their friends learn about plants.

a, b

Attitude is everything

1 How do we take care of plants? Tick (✓) the correct behaviour.

a 
Water plants.

b 
Let plants have sunlight and fresh air.

c 
Put plants in a cupboard.

d 
Pick wild flowers and plants.

e 
Step on plants.

2 How do you feel when you breathe like a tree? Circle the word and draw a face.

a sad
b happy
c calm
d worried

52

Pupils' own answers

Cultivated: strawberry, pine tree, cotton

Wild: dandelion, algae

This activity gives pupils practice of *Pre-A1 Starters* Listening Part 1.

Now I know

Assessment link

Go to page 84 for more activities.

1 Listen and draw lines to the pictures.

cultivated | wild

2 Draw a plant and label the parts.

roots leave stem flower

I am Aristotle.
I studied and classified plants.

Chant
Plants are useful

53

Pupils' own answers

UNIT 4
PAGE 53

Objective:

Pupils will review the content of the unit and read about Aristotle.

Key vocabulary

algae, cotton, cultivated, dandelion, flower, leaves, roots, stem, strawberries, trees, wild

Warm up

Sing the song *I am a plant*. Hand out a gap-fill copy of the words (with *roots, stem, leaves* and *seeds* missing). Pupils listen and complete.

Main concepts

- Read the Activity 1 rubric together. Check that pupils remember the meaning of *cultivated* and *wild*. Play the audio twice, pausing as necessary.
- Read the Activity 2 rubric together. Pupils draw, label and compare pictures. Vote for the best picture!
- As a class, look at the portrait of Aristotle and read the information.

Learn more

- Pupils choose a plant at home to watch and record its progress.
- Go to page 84 for more activities.
- Pupils can now put their fingerprint in the passport on page 5.

UNIT 4 LET'S REVIEW PAGE 84

Find the right words answers

1

a It's a beautiful flower.

b It's a tall tree.

c It's a green leaf.

d It isn't a healthy plant.

2

a It hasn't got a flower.

b It has got lots of leaves.

c It has got a thick trunk.

d It hasn't got a stem.

Look back answers

1

a 1

b 3

c 2

2

a chamomile

b strawberries

c trees

d cotton

This activity gives pupils practice of *Pre-A1 Starters* Reading and Writing Part 3.

UNIT 4 TRACKLIST

Track 30	Page 43, Song *I am a plant*
Track 31	Page 44, *Do we eat flowers? Listen and trace the lines.* Listening activity
Track 32	Page 46, *Is grass always green?*
Track 33	Page 48, *Do all plants need us to look after them?*
Track 34	Page 50, *Where does paper come from?*
Track 35	Page 53, *Listen and draw lines to the pictures.* Listening activity
Track 36	Page 53, Chant *Plants are useful*
Track 37	Page 53, *I am Aristotle* Character
Track 57	Page 85, *Listen and write the numbers.* Listening activity
Track 60	Page 92, *Story 2. Listen and read.*

Story 2

Topic: Plants and animals

Summary: Little Darwin is telling Little Curie and Little Linnaeus about his trip around the world. He explains where he went and what he saw, and Little Curie shows how her plant is healthy again. Little Linnaeus realises plants and animals have the same needs because both are living things.

Pupils listen to the story and complete *Now I know* activities on pages 92 and 93.

Now I know story answers

1 3, 2, 1

2 fish, polar bear, plant

5

I'M ALIVE!

Learning objectives

By the end of this unit, your pupils will have achieved a greater understanding of the following concepts:

- the differences between living and non-living things
- the life cycle of living things
- what living things need to survive

Competences

This unit covers the following competences:

- Linguistic competence
- Mathematical competence and basic competences in science and technology
- Digital competence
- Learning to learn
- Cultural awareness and expression

Key vocabulary

Stages of life: born, die, grow, reproduce

Human stages of life: adult, baby, boy, girl, old

What we need to live: air, food, water

Non-living things: ball, chair, cloud, rock, sand, sun

Cambridge English Qualifications practice

You will find *Pre-A1 Starters* activity types in the following exercises:

Pupil's Book, Page 86, Activity 2 – Reading and Writing Part 5

Activity Book, Page 28, Activity 6 – Reading and Writing Part 4

Activity Book, Page 29, Activity 9 – Reading and Writing Part 1

Activity Book, Page 29, Activity 10 – Reading and Writing Part 4

Activity Book, Page 31, Activity 14 – Reading and Writing Part 5

Throughout this unit, you will find the following *Pre-A1 Starters* vocabulary:

angry, animal, baby, ball, boy, can, chair, classroom, do, girl, fish, food, fun, garden, go, happy, know, listen, live, look, make, meat, old, people, person, photo, sad, sand, see, sun, thing, tree, try, water

Materials needed for *projects*:

- Control plant from Unit 4, plastic container, artificial flower, soil
- Pictures of animals
- Notebooks/paper, photos of pupils as babies and age 3/4

Materials needed for other activities:

- decorations (glitter, beads), doll, glue, plastic bottle with lid, plastic flower, soft-toy animal

Experiment

The main project, Steps 1 and 2, will provide your pupils with the opportunity to see the difference between a living and non-living thing. They will use the *Control plant* from Unit 4, alongside an artificial flower, to see how one grows and develops, while the other remains the same.

Mindful time

Each unit has a mindful time feature that encourages pupils to relate learning to their feelings and emotions, their relationships with classmates, and their well-being.

In this unit, pupils learn to be aware of the different sensations things around them can create.

Digital Lab +

- Interactive activities
- Flashcards: plants and animals
- Song: *I'm alive*
- Chant: *Is it living?*
- Video documentary: *Living and non-living things*

UNIT 5
PAGES 54–55

Objective:

The opening spread will raise pupils' awareness of the differences between living and non-living things.

Key vocabulary

alive, coconut, living-things, non-living things

Warm up

Show pupils a plastic flower, a soft-toy animal and a doll. Ask *Are they alive? How do you know? Are you alive? How do you know?* Tell them that we can classify the things in our world as living and non-living, and that they will learn about this in this unit.

Main concepts

- Sing the song *I'm alive*. Encourage pupils to create actions for the song.
- Elicit the key ideas about life in the song: breathing, moving, growing, eating and drinking, and ask *Do you breathe? Do you move? Are you growing? Are you taller now than when you were a baby? Do you drink and eat every day?*
- Look at the opening spread. Ask pupils what they can see. Encourage them to use the structure *I can see …* Look at the questions on the page and encourage pupils to discuss their thoughts. Ask *Why is it important for us to eat?*

I can see two coconuts, a pear and some orange juice.

Mindful time

This Mindful time activity can be done in the playground or in the classroom. In the classroom, pupils should be conscious of the temperature of the room and the feel of the objects around them. They should touch different surfaces: a table, a wall, the floor, etc. and describe how it feels. In the playground, pupils should be conscious of the weather and the sounds around them. Can they feel the wind in their hair/the sun on their faces, etc?

Yes, they are.

He is acting.

He's eating and drinking.

Learn more

Tell pupils you will say *Living* or *Non-living* and they should touch something in the classroom. They have to touch something or someone different every time.

Song

The song explains what humans, plants and animals do that makes them living things, e.g. breathing, moving, eating and drinking, and growing.

Documentary

The documentary provides further clarification of what makes a living thing, and the differences between living and non-living things.

UNIT 5
PAGE 56

Objective:

Pupils will learn that plants are living things, what plants need and their life cycle.

Key vocabulary

air, born, die, food, grow, plant, reproduce, sunflower, water

Warm up

Say *Let's be a sunflower*. Demonstrate for pupils a mime of a sunflower opening up to the sun and then following it as it changes position in the sky. Ask pupils to copy.

Main concepts

- Ask *Do plants live forever?* Clarify as necessary and elicit that plants have a life cycle. Read the life cycle with pupils or play the audio and have them listen and read, pointing to the correct picture as they listen.
- Ask pupils if they can remember from the previous unit what plants need to live. Get them to point out the words and images on the page: *food, water, air*.

Learn more

- Read the Fun Fact. Ask *Do people use sunlight to make their food?* (We need sunlight because plants need sunlight. Without it, we can't grow crops to eat.)
- Ask pupils to colour the sunflower.

No, they don't.

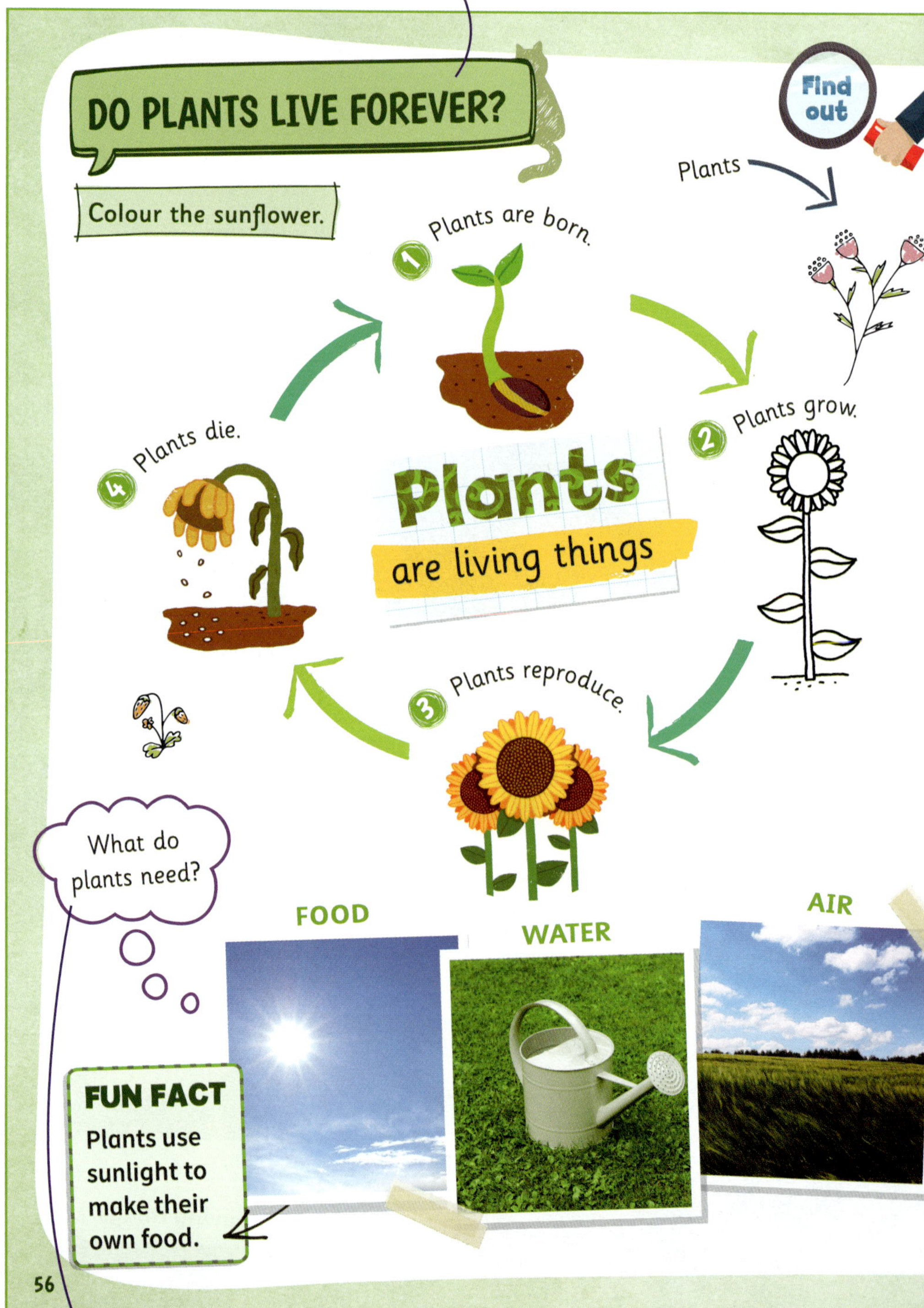

food, water and air

Project Step 1

Try it out

Let's make a crazy garden!

1 More plants! Take the *Control plant* from Unit four.

2 In the same plastic container, plant a plastic flower next to the *Control plant*.

Observe!
What do you think will happen?

MY DICTIONARY

born

grow

reproduce

die

What have I learnt?

Plants are ____________, they ____________, ____________ and ____________.

Plants are living things.

Plants are born, they grow, reproduce and die.

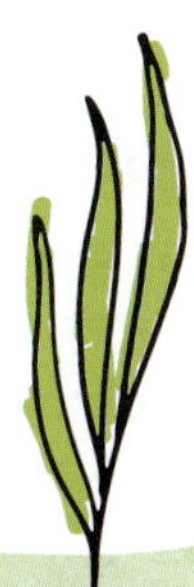

UNIT 5
PAGE 57

Objective:

Pupils will make a prediction about any differences between a real and an artificial plant.

Key vocabulary

born, die, grow, reproduce

Warm up

Sing *I'm alive* with actions.

Main concepts

- Say *Let's make a crazy garden!* In small groups, guide pupils through the steps. Each group should have a control plant and an artificial flower.
- Get them to form hypotheses by asking *Are the plants in the container different? Will the plastic flower grow? Will the control plant grow?* Display the questions and pupils' ideas in a chart to refer back to.
- Tell pupils that trees can live for a very long time and display pictures of some of them e.g. Methuselah, over 4,800 years old!

Learn more

- Read *My dictionary* as a class. Ask pupils to find the sticker and trace the words.
- Ask pupils to read and complete the *What have I learnt?* box individually.

UNIT 5
PAGE 58

Objective:

Pupils will understand that animals are living things too, what they need to live and their life cycles.

Key vocabulary

air, animal, baby, born, die, eat, food, gorillas, grow, herbivores, meat, need, reproduce, salad, water

Warm up

Ask *Do animals have families?* Ask for examples, e.g. dogs have *puppies*, etc. Pupils may have a puppy or kitten, or other pet, at home. Encourage them to talk about them.

Main concepts

- Look at and read the animal life cycle with pupils or play the audio, and have them point to each stage.
- Ask *What do animals need to live?*
- Say *How many baby animals can you see?* Get pupils to circle them.
- Read the Fun Fact. Explain as necessary.
- Point out and read the hidden feature instruction. Pupils find the kitten.

Learn more

Play the game: *Who is my mum/dad?* Show pupils photos of baby animals and ask them to guess which animal it is.

3 – 2 baby gorillas, 1 puppy

Yes, they do.

DO ANIMALS HAVE FAMILIES?

Find out

How many baby animals can you see? Circle.

Animals

Animals are living things.

1 Animals are born.

2 Animals grow.

3 Animals reproduce.

4 Animals die.

What do animals need?

FOOD

WATER

AIR

FUN FACT

Gorillas are herbivores, they don't eat meat.

I want a salad!

Find the kitten hidden in the unit

58

The kitten is on page 56, behind the title.

food, water and air

Mini-project

What's in the box?

1 Animals! Let's make an animal poster.

2 Draw the things animals need. Make a poster and show it to other groups!

Try it out

My Dictionary

What have I learnt?

Animals need ____________, ____________ and ____________.
Animals are ____________ ____________.

59

Animals need food, water and air.
Animals are living things.

Objective:

Pupils will reflect on and consolidate their knowledge of what animals need to live.

Key vocabulary

air, food, living things, water

Warm up

Play *Hangman* with baby animal names, e.g. kitten.

Main concepts

- Books closed. Show pupils the box and ask *What's in the box? – Animals!* Give clues such as: *It's a living thing. It needs air, water and food.*
- Say *Let's make an animal poster!* Go through the instructions with the class. Pupils complete the task in groups.
- Ask *Do animals need the same as plants?* Get them to check by looking at page 56.

Learn more

- Read *My dictionary* as a class. Ask pupils to find the sticker and trace the words.
- Ask pupils to read and complete the *What have I learnt?* box individually.
- Pupils find out which animals live the longest. They share their findings in the next lesson.

UNIT 5
PAGE 60

Objective:

Pupils will understand that people are living things, what people need to live and their life cycle.

Key vocabulary

air, baby, born, boy, food, get old, girl, grow, need, people, person, reproduce, second, water, world

Warm up

Say *Are you alive? – Yes! Are you a living or non-living thing? – Living!* Sing *I'm alive!* and do the actions.

Main concepts

- Read or listen to the three stages of life with pupils. Check comprehension *What happens when we grow? – We get bigger/older*, etc.
- Ask pupils to think about the life cycles of plants, animals and people and what they need to live. *Are they the same or different?* You could ask pupils to look back in the unit to check. Elicit *They are the same because they are all living things.*
- Ask pupils to circle the oldest person on the page. Then read the Fun Fact together.

Learn more

Ask pupils what else people need to survive or live a long life, e.g. shelter, sleep, exercise.

Yes, we do.

DO WE CHANGE AS WE GROW?

Find out

Circle the oldest person on the page.

People

People are living things!

1 People are born.

2 People grow.

3 People reproduce and get old.

FUN FACT

A baby is born in the world every three seconds.

What do you need to live?

FOOD

WATER

AIR

60

food, water and air

Mini-project

The time of my life!

1 Make a table for the different stages of your life.

2 Add your photos. Draw yourself in the future. Do you look the same?

Try it out

MY DICTIONARY

baby

boy

girl

adult

What have I learnt?

When you are born, you are a ___________.
You grow into a ___________ or a ___________.
You keep growing and become an ___________.

Draw your favourite toy now and in the future! Is it different?

61

When you are born, you are a baby. You grow into a boy or a girl. You keep growing and become an adult.

UNIT 5
PAGE 61

Objective:

Pupils will think about how they have grown from baby to child and imagine what they will be like as adults.

Key vocabulary

adult, baby, boy, future, girl, stage

Warm up

Ask pupils *What's the earliest memory you have?* Provide an example if necessary. Then ask *How are you different now?*

Main concepts

- In groups, allow pupils some time to show each other their photos.
- Ask *What will you look like when you are an adult?* Elicit answers and encourage imagination. Ask *What do you want to do when you are an adult?* Elicit answers and provide examples if necessary.
- As a class, read through the instructions. Pupils complete the task.
- Invite pupils to show and explain their table to the class/small groups.

Learn more

- Read *My dictionary* as a class. Ask pupils to find the sticker and trace the words.
- Ask pupils to read and complete the *What have I learnt?* box individually.

UNIT 5
PAGE 62

Objective:

Pupils will identify and explain the differences between living and non-living things.

Key vocabulary

ball, chair, cloud, grow, non-living, rock, sand castle, sun

Warm up

Sing the chant *Is it living?*

Main concepts

- Blow a balloon up and say *A balloon grows. Is it living?* Elicit answers and reasons.
- Pupils look at the page and find non-living things. Read the two sentences and ask pupils to point at each object. Ask *How do we know these are non-living things?*
- In groups, ask each group to name one non-living thing in the classroom. Start a list on the board for each group. When the groups can't name anything else, the longest list is the winner.
- Do the Mindful time activity.

Learn more

Draw a chalk line on the floor. On one side write *living*, on the other *non-living*. Shout out the name of something living or non-living. Pupils jump to the correct side. If they are wrong, they are out. The last one in is the winner.

No, they don't.

Accept all suitable answers.

Project Step 2

Circle the correct answer.

Let's look at the crazy garden!

1 Are the plants in the container different?	Yes (circled)	No
2 Does the plastic flower grow?	Yes	No (circled)
3 Does the *Control plant* grow?	Yes (circled)	No

Which one is a living thing? Why?

the control plant, because it needs air, water and food to live, and it grows

What have I learnt?

There are many ________-________ things.
Chairs, ____________ and ____________ are non-living things.

There are many non-living things. Chairs, clouds and rocks are non-living things.

Try it out

My DICTIONARY

non-living things

chairs

clouds

rocks

63

UNIT 5
PAGE 63

Objective:

Pupils will observe the garden from Step 1 and arrive at a conclusion.

Key vocabulary

chairs, clouds, non-living things, rocks

Warm up

Use the plastic flower, soft toy and doll to review the differences between living and non-living things. Elicit that living things need water, food and air.

Main concepts

- As a class, go through the questions 1–3. Then ask pupils to examine their crazy gardens and circle the correct answer.
- Pupils should then think about the final speech bubble question. Ask for ideas from the class and discuss any differences in opinion.
- Invite pupils to present their group's container and to explain the differences between the control plant and the plastic flower.

Learn more

- Read *My dictionary* as a class. Ask pupils to find the sticker and trace the words.
- Ask pupils to read and complete the *What have I learnt?* box individually.

UNIT 5
PAGE 64

Objective:

Pupils will think about their feelings and create a tool to help them calm down.

Key vocabulary

angry, beads, bottle, calm down, glitter, glue, noisy, sad, shake, top

Warm up

In pairs/small groups, ask pupils to tell each other about situations which make them feel angry, sad, happy, etc.

Main concepts

- Write *Calm down* on the board. Ask if anyone knows what it means. Elicit answers and clarify.
- Say *Let's make a calm down bottle*. Read through the instructions. Assist pupils in making their *calm down* bottles.
- Ask *What is the calm down bottle for? Why do we shake it?* Accept ideas and clarify. Then, look at Activity 2 together.

Learn more

- Ask pupils to think of situations in the past when they could have used their *calm down* bottle.
- Do the Mindful time activity.

Attitude is everything

1 Let's make a ***calm down bottle***!

1 Get your materials ready.

2 Put glue in the bottle and paint.

3 Add glitter and beads.

4 Add water.

5 Put the top on.

6 Shake it!

… and breathe!

2 Use the ***calm down bottle*** to feel calm when …

you are angry.

you are sad.

the classroom is noisy.

living things: fish, person, tree

non-living things: rock, sand, window

Now I know

Assessment link

Go to page 86 for more activities.

1 Classify the following things.

tree

rock

window

person

fish

sand

living things	non-living things
______	______
______	______
______	______

2 Listen and draw a living and non-living thing.

I am Carl Linnaeus.

I was a scientist and I gave names to groups of living things.

Chant

Is it living?

a sunflower and a rock

UNIT 5
PAGE 65

Objective:

Pupils will review the content of the unit and read about Carl Linnaeus.

Key vocabulary

fish, living, non-living, person, rock, sand, scientist, thing, tree, window

Warm up

Sing the unit chant and song with actions.

Main concepts

- Read the instructions for Activity 1. Check comprehension by asking a volunteer to explain. Pupils complete the task.
- Read the instructions for Activity 2. Check comprehension then play the audio twice, pausing as necessary. Pupils compare their drawings. Ask *What did you draw? – A sunflower and a rock.*
- Together, look at the portrait of Carl Linnaeus and read the information.

Learn more

- Pupils count and name the living things in their homes.
- Go to page 86 for more activities.
- Pupils can now put their fingerprint in the passport on page 5.

UNIT 5 LET'S REVIEW PAGE 86

Find the right words **answers**

1

a There is

b There are

c There are

d There is

This activity gives pupils practice of *Pre-A1 Starters* Reading and Writing Part 5.

2

a strawberry

b four

c wood (or plastic)

d seeds

Look back **answers**

1

1 are born

2 grow

3 reproduce

4 die

This activity gives pupils practice of *Pre-A1 Starters* Reading and Writing Part 4.

2

green: a, c, d

red: b, e, f

UNIT 5 TRACKLIST

6

FEELINGS LAB

Learning objectives

By the end of this unit, your pupils will have achieved a greater understanding of the following concepts:

- identity and personal autonomy
- analysing your own feelings and respect for others' feelings
- taking responsibility for what you say and do
- good habits at home and at school

Competences

This unit covers the following competences:

- Linguistic competence
- Mathematical competence and basic competences in science and technology
- Digital competence
- Learning to learn
- Cultural awareness and expression
- Social and civic competences

Key vocabulary

Self-description: clever, great, help, kind, nice, opinion, person, share

Friendship: be honest, bully, play fair, take care of

Good habits at school: Can I help you?, help each other, say thank you/please/well done, take care of the materials, try your best, work hard

Good habits at home: get my schoolbag ready, keep calm, listen to others, make my bed, respect my family, tidy up my room

Cambridge English Qualifications practice

You will find *Pre-A1 Starters* activity types in the following exercises:

Pupil's Book, Page 88, Activity 2 – Reading and Writing Part 5

Pupil's Book, Page 89, Activity 2 – Reading and Writing Part 4

Activity Book, Page 33, Activity 3 – Reading and Writing Part 5

Activity Book, Page 35, Activity 7 – Reading and Writing Part 4

Throughout this unit, you will find the following *Pre-A1 Starters* vocabulary:

be, bed, can, class, classmate, colour, do, family, find, friend, get, give, go, good, great, happy, home, know, like, listen, make, mirror, name, nice, person, picture, play, please, point, put, room, say, thank you, tick, train, try, well done, what, write

Materials needed for *projects*:

- Bowl, crayons, markers, paper, pencils, scissors, shoe boxes, stickers
- Crayons, pencils

Materials needed for other activities:

- Crayons, markers, paper, pencil, scissors, string

Project

The main project, Steps 1–3, will provide your pupils with the opportunity to get to know themselves better. It will also build pupils' confidence as they see themselves through their own and their classmates' eyes.

Mindful time

Each unit has a mindful time feature that encourages pupils to relate learning to their feelings and emotions, their relationships with classmates, and their well-being.

In this unit, the mindful routine focuses on pupils' awareness, concentration and hand-eye coordination.

Digital Lab +

- Interactive activities
- Flashcards: share, play, make the bed
- Song: *Best friends forever*
- Chant: *I am a star*
- Video documentary: *Good choices*

UNIT 6
PAGES 66–67

Objective:

In the opening spread, pupils will think about and identify feelings. They will think about relationships with others, good habits at school and what it means to work in a team.

Key vocabulary

choices, feelings, forever, friends, good, happy, lab, mirrors, pay attention, scientist, share, together, work

Warm up

Ask pupils *Do you have a best friend?* Accept responses – some pupils may have more than one. Ask *What is special about your best friend?* Help with vocabulary and write some answers/adjectives on the board.

Main concepts

- Sing *Best friends forever*. Get pupils to dance in pairs/threes and do the actions together. Ask *Why is he/she a good friend?* and elicit the key ideas from the song.
- Ask pupils to look at the picture in the spread. *What can you see?* Then, go through the questions on the page as a class. Encourage pupils to voice their ideas.
- Watch the documentary *Good choices*. After watching, ask pupils what it was about. Accept any appropriate responses.

No, he isn't.

No, she isn't.

Mindful time
Pupils should do the routine in pairs, facing each other. First, they look at each other's hair, ears, eyes, nose and mouth. Then, one is the mirror: they must imitate the movements and facial expressions that their partner makes for one minute. Then pupils swap roles and repeat.

No, they aren't.

Yes, they are.

Learn more

Play *Find a friend*. On a piece of paper, pupils write their 5 favourite things, e.g. food/drink, sport, film, book, colour. They go round the class asking different people *What's your favourite ...?* When someone answers the same as them, they write the name down. Whichever name they write the most is their new friend!

Song

The song talks about the essence and qualities of a friendship.

Documentary

The documentary makes pupils aware of the choices they make at home and school with a focus on good values.

UNIT 6
PAGE 68

Objective:

Pupils will learn about the positive qualities that they and other people can have.

Key vocabulary

clever, great, help, kind, nice, opinion, share

Tip

Before the Warm up, ask pupils if they can remember the adjectives used in the song to describe people. Write them on the board.

Warm up

In pairs, pupils sing *Best friends forever* and do the actions.

Main concepts

- As a class, look at the photos and read the speech bubbles. Check comprehension by asking pupils to tell you what they think it means. Then, say *Stand up if you are kind, clever, etc.* Make sure all pupils stand up every time! Everyone can shout out *We can all be great!* together.
- Go through the instruction together. Pupils complete the task.

Learn more

In pairs, pupils roleplay the situations in the photos, practising the sentences.

Yes, I am!

ARE YOU A GREAT PERSON?

Find out

Write your name on the star. Colour it.

I can share.

I am nice.

I can give my opinion.

I am clever.

I can help.

I am kind.

We can all be great!

68

Project Step 1

Try it out

Let's make a postbox.

1 Make and decorate your postbox.

2 Write a nice message for yourself and post it!

I am kind.

I can share.

MY DICTIONARY

clever

help

kind

nice

share

What have I learnt?

I am ________, ________ and ________.
I can ________ and ________.

I am clever, kind and nice. I can help and share.

UNIT 6
PAGE 69

Objective:

Pupils will complete Step 1 of the project and think about their positive qualities.

Key vocabulary

clever, help, kind, nice, share

Warm up

- Books closed. Ask pupils if they can remember the sentences from the previous lesson, *I am clever,* etc. Write them on the board.
- Alternatively, ask a pair to the front of the class, whisper a sentence to them, then they act it out for the others to guess.

Main concepts

- As a class, go through the instructions. Pupils complete the task. Provide help as necessary with cutting the box and the messages.
- Encourage pupils to write messages for members of their family. They can post them in their boxes and share them with family when they take their boxes home.

Learn more

- Read *My dictionary* as a class. Ask pupils to find the sticker and trace the words.
- Ask pupils to read and complete the *What have I learnt?* box individually.

UNIT 6
PAGE 70

Objective:

Pupils will think about how to be a good friend.

Key vocabulary

be honest, best, bully, different, friend, good, play fair, say sorry, take care of

Warm up

Books closed. Ask pupils *What makes a good friend?* Write ideas on the board. Ask *Are you a good friend?* You can reflect on these ideas at the end of the lesson.

Main concepts

- Ask pupils to look at the photos and captions. Ask them what they think is happening in the photos.
- Play the audio, then play the audio again, pausing after each phrase for pupils to repeat.
- Look at the picture and phrase *Different, but best friends.* Ask pupils what they think it means.

Learn more

- In small groups, give each group one of the qualities, e.g. be honest. Pupils create a short scene to act out the quality.
- Return to the ideas from the Warm up. Add any more pupils have learnt and ask pupils to think about them. Ask again *Are you a good friend?*

Yes, I am!

ARE YOU A GOOD FRIEND?

Find out

Listen and point.

Play fair.

Don't be a bully.

Take care of little ones.

Different, but best friends.

Be honest.

70

Project Step 2

Try it out

Write a message for your friend.

1 In your class, put all of your names in a bowl.

2 Take a name and write a positive message for that person.

3 Turn the paper over and draw your friend as a superhero.

My Dictionary

be honest

bully

play fair

take care of little ones

What have I learnt?

To be a good friend:
play ______________, don't be a ______________,
take ______________ of little ones
and be ______________.

Put the message in your friend's postbox!

To be a good friend: play fair, don't be a bully, take care of little ones and be honest.

UNIT 6
PAGE 71

Objective:

In Step 2 of the project, pupils will think about the positive things they can say to a friend.

Key vocabulary

be honest, bully, kind, play fair, share, take care of little ones

Warm up

Ask pupils to think about a time that they helped a friend. Give them time to think, then elicit responses. Ask them to tell the class.

Main concepts

- As a class, read through the instructions. Then, pupils each write their name on a piece of paper and put it in the bowl. Each pupil takes a name (not their own!) and completes the task. Provide help with writing as necessary.
- When they've finished, they post the messages in their friends' postboxes.
- Pupils tell a partner good things about their best friend/one of their friends.

Learn more

- Read *My dictionary* as a class. Ask pupils to find the sticker and trace the words.
- Ask pupils to read and complete the *What have I learnt?* box individually.

UNIT 6
PAGE 72

Objective:

Pupils will think about the qualities of a good classmate and good behaviour at school.

Key vocabulary

brain, classmate, good, help each other, please, say, take care of classroom materials, thank you, together, train, try your best, well done, work hard

Warm up

Ask pupils *What makes a good classmate?* Add ideas to the board. Ask *Are you a good classmate?* You can revisit these ideas at the end of the lesson.

Main concepts

- Ask pupils to look at the main picture and describe what they see.
- Ask the two questions to the class and elicit responses. Ask them *why* they like (or don't like) working together.
- Go through the advice lists, discussing what pupils do/don't do.
- Pupils point to the super classmates and explain why.
- Look at the cartoon. Explain the brain is a muscle.

Learn more

Pupils think of other ways to be a good classmate, e.g. put the books away, tidy the chairs, etc. Then they share with the class.

Yes, I am!

Accept any appropriate answers.

ARE YOU A GOOD CLASSMATE?

Find out

Point to the super classmates in the picture.

When do you say *please*?

Do you like working together?

Train your brain by working hard!

ALWAYS TRY TO ...

- work hard.
- try your best.
- help each other.
- take care of classroom materials.

SAY ...

- please
- thank you
- well done!
- Can I help you?

72

Accept any appropriate answers.

Accept any appropriate answers.

Project Step 3

Try it out

Let's write a message for the class.

1 Write a positive message for the whole class.

2 Share your messages with your classmates!

We help each other.

My Dictionary

help each other

say well done

try your best

work hard

What have I learnt?

Super classmates ______________ hard, ______________ their best and ______________ each other.
Super classmates say ______________ ______________.

Super classmates work hard, try their best and help each other. Super classmates say *well done*.

73

UNIT 6
PAGE 73

Objective:

In Step 3 of the project, pupils will think about how they work together as a team.

Key vocabulary

help each other, say well done, try your best, work hard

Warm up

Play a game of *Hangman* to review the words and phrases learnt in this unit. Add them to a list on the board for pupils to refer to.

Main concepts

- Say *Let's write a message for the class.*
- To have a variety of messages, encourage pupils to refer to the examples on the board and to look back through the unit. Pupils can also include new ideas.
- Pupils complete the task and share with the class.
- As an extension, pupils can create a message poster, displayed on the wall.

Learn more

- Read *My dictionary* as a class. Ask pupils to find the sticker and trace the words.
- Ask pupils to read and complete the *What have I learnt?* box individually.

UNIT 6
PAGE 74

Objective:

Pupils will learn about good habits and helping at home, and will reflect on their relationships with their families.

Key vocabulary

find, get my schoolbag ready, help, hidden, home, keep calm, listen to others, make my bed, respect my family, schoolbag, tidy up my room, treasures

Warm up

Sing the chant *I am a star*. Do the actions. Ask *Why are you a star?* and elicit the things they do in the song, e.g. *Because I tidy up.*

Main concepts

- Books closed. Ask pupils *Do you help at home? What do you do?* Write answers on the board.
- Look at the examples on the page and ask who does each thing. Check comprehension by asking for examples from individual pupils.
- Say *What else do you do to help at home?* Pupils draw themselves helping at home. Help with ideas and point out the examples on the board.

Learn more

Together, read *Tidy up your room and find your treasures.* Ask *Have you ever found any treasure in your room?*

Yes, I do!

DO YOU HELP AT HOME?

Find out

Draw another thing you do at home.

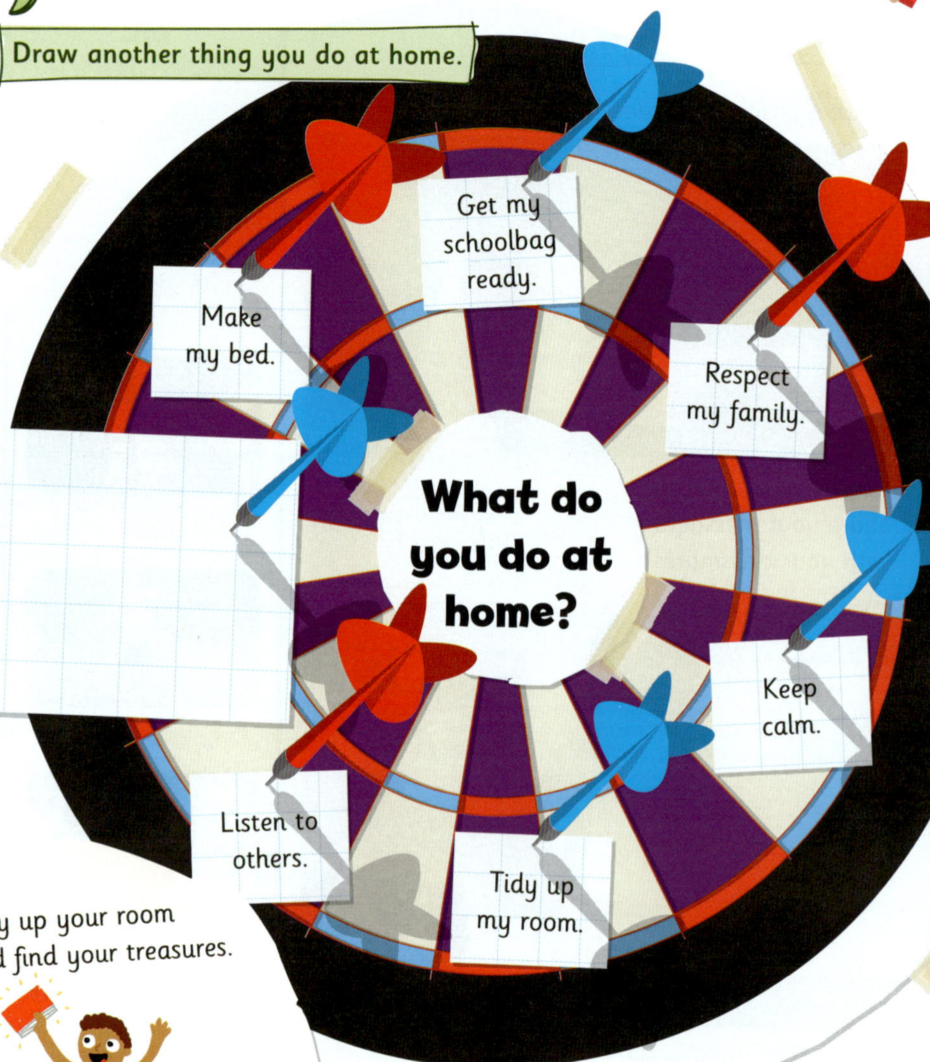

Tidy up your room and find your treasures.

Find the schoolbag hidden in the unit!

The schoolbag is behind *My dictionary* on page 69.

74

Mini-project

Work in groups and complete the table.
Colour the boxes to show what you do at home.

Try it out

Name	I make my bed.	I get my schoolbag ready.	I respect my family.	I keep calm.

Do you keep calm?

Yes, I do. / No, I don't.

What have I learnt?

In the morning, I ______________ my bed
and ______________ my schoolbag ready.
I ______________ my family and
keep ______________ .

In the morning, I make my bed and get my schoolbag ready.
I respect my family and keep calm.

My Dictionary

get my schoolbag ready

keep calm

make my bed

respect my family

75

UNIT 6
PAGE 75

Objective:

Pupils will complete a survey about how they help at home.

Key vocabulary

get my schoolbag ready, keep calm, make my bed, respect my family

Warm up

A pupil mimes an activity from the previous lesson, e.g. make my bed, and the others guess.

Main concepts

- Write *I make my bed.* on the board. Ask *How do we ask the question?* Guide pupils toward the answer *Do you make your bed?* and the answer *Yes, I do. / No, I don't.* and write them on the board. Do this for each activity in the table.
- Pupils ask each other the questions. If the answer is *Yes,* they colour the square.
- Pupils look for any empty squares and think about what more they need to do at home and set goals.

Learn more

- Read *My dictionary* as a class. Ask pupils to find the sticker and trace the words.
- Ask pupils to read and complete the *What have I learnt?* box individually.

UNIT 6
PAGE 76

Objective:

Pupils will reflect on their good points and connect with their feelings.

Key vocabulary

cut out, feel, glue, hang up, message, postbox, star

Warm up

Review feelings. Elicit the words from pupils and write them on the board, e.g. happy, sad, calm, angry, etc. Say *How are you feeling today?*

Main concepts

- As a class, read through the instructions for Activity 1. Pupils should read through all their messages before choosing a favourite. When the stars have been hung up, invite each pupil to read out their message.
- Look at Activity 2. Check that pupils can identify the feeling in each photo. Allow them to add another feeling if they wish. Encourage pupils to say why they feel this way.

Learn more

In teams, ask pupils to remember as many examples as they can about being a great person, friend or classmate, and helping at home. Give a point for each one the teams shout out.

Attitude is everything

1 Make your star.

1 Choose one of the messages from your postbox.

2 Glue it to your star.

3 Colour and cut out your star.

4 Hang it up in the classroom.

2 How do you feel when you read your messages? Tick (✓).

Why do you feel like this?

76

b, c, d, e

Now I know

Assessment link
Go to page 88 for more activities.

1 Tick (✓) the good choices.

a

I don't play fair. ☐

b

I'm not a bully. ☐

c

I work hard. ☐

d

I make my bed. ☐

e

I help others. ☐

2 Listen and complete the good behaviours list.

- I r__________ my family.
- I l__________ to others.
- I am n__________.
- I make my b__________.
- I t__________ my room.

YOU ARE A SUPER CLASSMATE!

Chant
I am a star

I am Marie Curie.
Thanks to me, doctors can use x-rays!

I respect my family.
I listen to others.
I am nice.
I make my bed.
I tidy up my room.

UNIT 6
PAGE 77

Objective:

Pupils will review the content of the unit and read about Marie Curie.

Key vocabulary

bully, choices, good, help others, listen to others, make my bed, nice, play fair, respect my family, room, tidy up, work hard, x-ray

Warm up

Perform the chant and the song.

Main concepts

- Read the instructions for Activity 1 and check comprehension. Pupils compare answers with a classmate.
- Go through the list and encourage pupils to complete the gaps before they listen. Don't give them the answers. Play the audio twice. Pupils compare answers before checking as a class.
- Look at the photo of Marie Curie and read the information.

Learn more

- Together, read the biography of Marie Curie from *Good Night Stories for Rebel Girls* by Elena Favilli and Francesca Cavallo.
- Go to page 88 for more activities.
- Pupils can now put their fingerprint in the passport on page 5.

UNIT 6 LET'S REVIEW PAGE 88

Find the right words answers

1

I am ...

clever, honest, kind (in any order)

I ...

listen, share, work hard (in any order)

2

a playing

b helping

c working

d listening

This activity gives pupils practice of *Pre-A1 Starters* Reading and Writing Part 5.

Look back answers

1

a Listen to others.

b Respect your family.

c Try your best.

d Keep calm.

2

a work

b bed

c schoolbag

d park

This activity gives pupils practice of *Pre-A1 Starters* Reading and Writing Part 4.

UNIT 6 TRACKLIST

Track 46	Page 67, Song *Best friends forever*
Track 47	Page 68, *Are you a great person?*
Track 48	Page 70, *Are you a good friend? Listen and point.* Listening activity
Track 49	Page 72, *Are you a good classmate?*
Track 50	Page 74, *Do you help at home?*
Track 51	Page 77, *Listen and complete the good behaviours list.* Listening activity
Track 52	Page 77, Chant *I am a star*
Track 53	Page 77, *I am Marie Curie* Character
Track 61	Page 94, *Story 3. Listen and read.*

Story 3

Topic: Characteristics of living and non-living things, and safety in a lab

Summary: Little Curie is working in her lab with Little Franklin and Little Aristotle. While she is explaining the differences between living and non-living things, Little Aristotle is distracted by a rock. He drops the rock on his foot and he learns the importance of being careful in a lab.

Pupils listen to the story and complete *Now I know* activities on pages 94 and 95.

Now I know story answers

1 3, 1, 2

2 Accept any correct answers which feature in the story

AUDIO SCRIPTS

UNIT 1

Track 02 Page 7, Mindful time

Take three deep breaths. You can close your eyes. Pay attention to the sounds.

Track 03 Page 7, Song *Body parts*

(*Chorus*) Body parts! Body parts!
Your body, my body
Everybody move your body!

Start with your head, to your right, to your left
Then wave your arms, up and down, up and down
(Chorus)

Tap your feet, one two three, one two three
Now turn around, but don't get dizzy!
(Chorus)

Track 07 Page 13, Listening activity

Listen and draw your monster.

My monster has got one mouth and six ears. My monster has got four eyes. Two eyes are blue and two eyes are green.

Track 09 Page 17, Listening activity

Listen and number the body parts.

1 leg
2 finger
3 tummy
4 head
5 arm
6 hand
7 bottom
8 foot

Track 11 Page 17, Chant *Five senses*

Five senses
I've got five senses
1, 2, 3, 4, 5!
I can smell
I can taste
And I can see
I can touch
I can hear
Everything around me!
Five senses
I've got five senses
1, 2, 3, 4, 5!

Track 54 Page 78, Listening activity.

Listen and circle the correct words.

a This is my tongue.
b This is my neck.
c These are my knees.
d These are my elbows.

UNIT 2

Track 12 Page 19, Song *I like healthy food!*

***(Chorus)* I like healthy food**
Like vegetables and fruit
Eating healthily
Is good for you and me!
It's Monday morning
I've got a tummy ache
Eating pizza
Chocolate and cake
(Chorus)

I miss my salad
And my chicken too
Yogurt for a snack
It's healthy, that's true!
(Chorus)

Track 17 Page 28, Listening activity

How does Lucy feel? Listen and tick.

Hi, I am Lucy! I feel happy today! I am having fun with my mum and sister.

Track 18 Page 29, Chant *Be healthy*

Wash your hands
With soap and water
Be healthy!
Brush your teeth
Nice and clean
Be healthy!
Have a shower
Don't take an hour
Be healthy!
Practise sport
Every day
Be healthy!
Sleep all night
You'll feel just right
Be healthy!

Track 55 Page 81, Listening activity

Listen and tick the box.

1 Which snack is healthy?

Boy: Mum, can I have a snack, please?
Mum: Yes, but you should have a healthy snack.
Boy: I'd like a donut.
Mum: No. Have a banana. Bananas are healthy.
Boy: Ok, then!

2 Which snack is unhealthy?

Mum: Annie, would you like a snack? We've got yoghurt and pears.
Annie: But I want crisps.
Mum: Crisps are unhealthy! Have a yoghurt!

3 How many times a day should you eat?

Boy: I'm really hungry.
Mum: I'm not surprised! You don't eat breakfast. You need to eat five times a day to stay healthy.

UNIT 3

Track 21 Page 31, Song *Move like an animal*

***(Chorus)* Move your body, move like an animal (x2)**

A fish can swim and swim
Swim like a fish
A polar bear walks like this
Walk like a polar bear
(Chorus)

A snake slithers all day
S-s-slither like a snake
And a puffin flies this way
Flap and fly like a puffin
(Chorus)

Your turn now! Show us how!
How do you move?
Your turn now! Show us how!
How do you move?
(Chorus)

Track 26 Page 38, Listening activity

Listen and circle the correct animal.

I am a bird and I can fly. I am a wild animal.

Track 27 Page 41, Listening activity

Listen and circle the invertebrates.

I can walk and I have got a skeleton. I am a cow.
I can swim and I have not got a skeleton. I am a jellyfish.
I can fly and I have not got a skeleton. I am a butterfly.
I can walk and I have got a skeleton. I am a dog.
I can walk but I have not got a skeleton. I am a crab.
I can slither and I have got a skeleton. I am a snake.

AUDIO SCRIPTS

Track 28 Page 41, Chant *Wild, domestic*

Wild or domestic?
Domestic or wild?
Dogs and cats ... are domestic
Pigs and sheep ... are domestic
Wild or domestic?
Domestic or wild?
Badgers and foxes ... are wild
Snakes and bats ... are wild
Wild or domestic?
Domestic or wild?

Track 56 Page 83, Listening activity

Listen and colour.

1

Female: Look, there are lots of living things. Colour the fox?
Girl: The fox?
Female: Yes. Have you got an orange pencil?
Girl: Yes, I have.
Female: Great, colour it with that pencil then.

2

Female: Can you see the fish?
Girl: Yes!
Female: Well done! Colour the fish now, please?
Girl: What colour?
Female: Would you like to colour them purple?
Girl: Yes!

3

Female: Now colour the bird that is flying.
Girl: The bird that is flying? OK.
Female: You can choose the colour!
Girl: Ok, I'll colour it brown!

4

Female: Can you see the trees?
Girl: I can see them.
Female: Good, make them green please.
Girl: Ok, I'm colouring the trees green, now.
Female: Great!

UNIT 4

Track 30 Page 43, Song *I am a plant*

(Chorus) I'm a plant, I'm a plant, take care of me (x2)

I've got roots and a stem
Come here and look at them!
(Chorus)

I've got leaves I use to breathe
I've got flowers, can you see?
(Chorus)

I've got lots of seeds too
New plants will grow soon
(Chorus)

Track 31 Page 44, Listening activity

Listen and trace the lines.

Do we eat flowers?
A plant can have a flower, a stem, leaves, roots.
Some plants grow from seeds.
I am a flower! Do you know my name?
I am a lettuce. I have lots of leaves! I was a baby before.
I am asparagus! I am a stem.
I am an onion. I am a root vegetable!

Track 35 Page 53, Listening activity

Listen and draw lines to the pictures.

Strawberries are cultivated plants. We grow them in gardens or fields.
Dandelions are wild plants. They grow everywhere.
Pine trees are cultivated and grow in fields.
Algae is wild and grows everywhere.

Track 36 Page 53, Chant *Plants are useful*

Plants are useful, plants are useful
Food! Apples, oranges and bananas
Clothes! T-shirts, trousers and skirts
Medicines! Have a chamomile tea
Wood! Sit on your chair
Plants are useful, plants are useful

Track 57 Page 85, Listening activity

Listen and write the numbers.

1 Grass is bendy. Wheat is grass, too.
2 A tree has got a thick trunk and lots of branches. Some trees give us fruit, too.
3 A bush has got a lot of woody stems. Some bushes give us fruit.

UNIT 5

Track 38 Page 55, Song *I'm alive*

***(Chorus)* We're alive, yes, we're alive!**
I'm alive, you're alive
We're alive, yes, we're alive!
We can breathe in and breathe out
Like animals and plants: we're alive
We can move our body up and down
Like animals and plants: we're alive
(Chorus)

We need water, food and air
Like animals and plants: we're alive
We are born, we grow and we get old
Like animals and plants: we're alive
(Chorus)

Track 43 Page 65, Listening activity

Listen and draw a living and non-living thing.

I am a living thing. I am a plant. I am a sunflower. I have got a green stem and a yellow flower.

I am a non-living thing. I am a rock. I am brown.

Track 44 Page 65, Chant *Is it living?*

Non-living, non-living, no, no non-living (x2)
A balloon grows more and more, is it living?
No, it isn't.
A cloud moves in the sky, is it living?
No it isn't.
A teddy bear has legs and arms, is it living?
No it's isn't.
A river flows really fast, is it living?
No, it isn't.
Non-living, non-living, no, no non-living (x2)

Track 58 Page 87, Listening activity

Circle the living things green and the non-living things red. Listen and check.

a People are living-things. People are born, grow, reproduce and get old.
b Rocks cannot reproduce. Rocks are non-living things.
c A starfish is a living thing. It is an invertebrate.
d Trees are living things. Trees grow and reproduce.
e Chairs cannot grow. Chairs are non-living things.
f TVs are not born. A TV is a non-living thing.

AUDIO SCRIPTS

UNIT 6

Track 46 Page 67, Song *Best friends forever*

(Chorus) **You're my best friend**
Best friends forever
I'll be there for you
For now and ever
Hold my hand, give me a smile
You are great, I like your style
(Chorus)

You say thank you, sorry, please
And you mean the world to me!
(Chorus)

You are clever, nice and kind
You share at school, you never mind
(Chorus)

Track 48 Page 70, Listening activity

Listen and point.

To be a good friend:
Play fair.
Don't be a bully.
Take care of little ones.
Be honest.

Track 51 Page 77 Listening activity

Listen and complete the good behaviours list.

I respect my family.
I listen to others.
I am nice.
I make my bed.
I tidy up my room.

Track 52 Page 77, Chant *I am a star*

I make my bed and I tidy up
That's why my family is so proud
I listen first and I work hard
That's why my family is so proud
I help others and respect my family
That's why my family is so proud
I make good choices and I try my best
That's why my family is so proud!

ACTIVITY BOOK ANSWERS

UNIT 1

1

a joint – elbow

b bones – hand

c muscles – leg

2

s	y	h	p	w	v	k	y	o
s	h	d	p	e	l	b	o	w
a	u	o	x	j	c	n	l	r
n	v	f	u	d	h	b	s	i
k	g	n	x	l	d	k	z	s
l	g	h	h	j	d	n	r	t
e	t	k	l	l	o	e	a	e
w	t	h	i	p	i	e	r	l
q	p	r	r	l	w	m	g	a

3

head – pink/purple

torso – yellow

limbs – green

4

a true

b false

c true

d true

5

a two

b one

c one

d two

e one

6

a chin

b eyes

c nose

d tongue

e mouth

This activity gives pupils practice of *Pre-A1 Starters* Reading and Writing Part 3.

7

as per AB instructions

8

Pupils' own answers

9

a ✔

b ✔

c ✗

d ✗

e ✗

10

a Joints

b torso

11

see – painting

smell – rubbish

taste – ice cream

touch – teddy bear

hear – ear phones

12

a touch

b smell

c hear

d taste

13

a eyes

b nose

c hands

d ears

ACTIVITY BOOK ANSWERS

UNIT 2

1
carbohydrates: bread, pasta, potatoes
proteins: meat, fish, eggs, nuts
fruit and vegetables: bananas, tomatoes, lettuce, oranges, etc.
fats: chocolate, butter, oil, etc.
dairy: milk, cheese, yoghurt, etc.

2
a fruit

b vegetable

c fruit

d vegetable

3
pasta

meat

milkshake

biscuits

orange

4
proteins – chicken

carbohydrates – bread

fruit and vegetables – banana; lettuce

dairy – yoghurt

fats – butter

5
a ✗

b ✓

c ✗

d ✗

e ✓

f ✗

This activity gives pupils practice of *Pre-A1 Starters* Reading and Writing Part 1.

6
Pupils' own answers

7
a breakfast

b snack

c lunch

d dinner

This activity gives pupils practice of *Pre-A1 Starters* Reading and Writing Part 3.

8
a five

b fruit and vegetables

9
a green

b red

c red

d green

10
muscles

healthy

heart

11
a teeth

b day

c hands

12
1 b

2 a

13
a crisps

b school

c yoghurt/sandwiches

d sandwiches/yoghurt

14
a angry

b sad

c happy

UNIT 3

1

a the Arctic

b ocean

c farm

d forest

2

fish

crab

3

a ✔

b ✗

c ✗

d ✔

This activity gives pupils practice of *Pre-A1 Starters* Reading and Writing Part 1.

4

Pupils' own answers

5

a walk

b fly

c slither

d swim

6

fly: puffin

walk: polar bear

slither: seal

swim: fish

7

a fish

b bird

c reptile

d mammal

e amphibian

This activity gives pupils practice of *Pre-A1 Starters* Reading and Writing Part 3.

8

yellow: dog, badger and squirrel

blue: salamanders and frog

9

hen

cow

snail

horse

penguin

10

Wild: badger, fox, owl

Domestic: cow, sheep, hen

11

a bird

b rainforest

c trees

d Koalas

This activity gives pupils practice of *Pre-A1 Starters* Reading and Writing Part 4.

12

a vertebrate

b slither

c reptile

d has not got

ACTIVITY BOOK ANSWERS

UNIT 4

1
a roots
b flower
c stem
d leaves
e seeds

2
a flower
b leaves
c stem
d roots

3
a ✗
b ✓
c ✗
d ✓
e ✗

This activity gives pupils practice of *Pre-A1 Starters* Reading and Writing Part 1.

4
a trunk
b branches
c Bushes
e Grass

This activity gives pupils practice of *Pre-A1 Starters* Reading and Writing Part 4.

5
a and c

6
a yes
b no
c yes
d no
e yes

This activity gives pupils practice of *Pre-A1 Starters* Reading and Writing Part 2.

7
a furniture
b food
c medicine
d clothes

8
a chamomile
b pine tree
c strawberry
d cotton

9
a, b, e

10
a true
b true
c false
d false

11
a and b

12
Red: boy playing football on plants; girl pulling off a leaf

Green: man watering the plants; man trimming the bush

UNIT 5

1
a plants

b animal

c people

2
1 Plants are born.

2 Plants grow.

3 Plants reproduce.

4 Plants die.

3
food, water, air (in any order)

4
a no

b yes

c yes

d no

5
a 3

b 1

c 2

6
a babies

b girl/boy

c girl/boy

d adults

e reproduce

This activity gives pupils practice of *Pre-A1 Starters* Reading and Writing Part 4.

7
mountain range

balloon fish

8
reproduce, grow, born, air, water, food

9
a ✔

b ✗

c ✔

d ✗

e ✔

This activity gives pupils practice of *Pre-A1 Starters* Reading and Writing Part 1.

10
A *lion* is a *living* thing because it needs *air/water,* food and *water/air* to live.

This activity gives pupils practice of *Pre-A1 Starters* Reading and Writing Part 4.

11
a the sun

b a chair

12

s	a	n	d	q	a	w
c	o	y	b	w	r	a
b	l	t	e	x	o	t
j	m	o	s	f	c	e
r	u	s	u	n	k	r
a	q	p	c	d	y	o

13
green: bird, two boys in a canoe, fisherman, reindeer, trees, fish

red: table and benches, cabin, canoe, mountain range, river, tents, waterfall

14
a two

b fishing

c two

This activity gives pupils practice of *Pre-A1 Starters* Reading and Writing Part 5.

15
Pupils' own answers

ACTIVITY BOOK ANSWERS

UNIT 6

1

a I am nice.

b I am clever.

c I can help.

2

bullying

quarrelling

3

a kitchen

b milk

c yes

d no

e no

This activity gives pupils practice of *Pre-A1 Starters* Reading and Writing Part 5.

4

a, c, d

5

Suggested answers:

With friends: play fair, be kind, listen to others

At school: play fair, be kind, listen to others

At home: get your schoolbag ready, listen to others

6

Pupils' own answers

7

a friend

b play

c words

d bully

e little ones

This activity gives pupils practice of *Pre-A1 Starters* Reading and Writing Part 4.

8

Name: pupils' own answers

My friend is kind and plays fair.

My friend helps me.

My friend always says thank you.

9

Suggested answers:

a ✔

b ✗

c ✔

d ✔

e ✔

10

the bedroom and the kitchen

11

l	j	s	h	a	r	e
l	i	f	b	m	p	g
r	e	s	p	e	c	t
n	e	e	t	v	y	c
d	s	f	h	e	l	p
z	i	a	y	p	n	m